T0319942

The Geography of Creativity

The Geography of Creativity

Gunnar Törnqvist

Department of Social and Economic Geography, Lund University, Sweden and The Royal Swedish Academy of Sciences

Translated by Ken Schubert

Edward Elgar
Cheltenham, UK • Northampton, MA, USA

Published by
Edward Elgar Publishing Limited
The Lypiatts
15 Lansdown Road
Cheltenham
Glos GL50 2JA
UK

Edward Elgar Publishing, Inc.
William Pratt House
9 Dewey Court
Northampton
Massachusetts 01060
USA

A catalogue record for this book
is available from the British Library

Library of Congress Control Number: 2011936423

ISBN 978 1 78100 150 9

Typeset by Servis Filmsetting Ltd, Stockport, Cheshire
Printed and bound by MPG Books Group, UK

Contents

List of figures   viii
List of tables   ix
Preface   x

1. Prologue   1
    1.1   Creativity   1
    1.2   Points of departure   3
2. Process   7
    2.1   Bisociation   7
    2.2   Lateral and vertical thinking   12
    2.3   Phases of a process   14
3. Person   17
    3.1   The creative child   17
    3.2   The creative class   18
    3.3   The original creator   20
    3.4   The entrepreneur   22
4. Place   25
    4.1   The concept of place   25
    4.2   Ancient and Renaissance cities   26
    4.3   The rise of modern cities   32
    4.4   Localized features in common   39
5. Metropolis   46
    5.1   Communication and cultural diversity   47
    5.2   Creative capital   50
    5.3   Breeding grounds of renewal   61

6.   The institutional milieu   63
     6.1   Form and size   64
     6.2   Can creativity and productivity
           be reconciled?   74
7.   The scientific revolution   78
     7.1   The great breakthrough   78
     7.2   The third mission   83
     7.3   Clusters and innovation systems   87
     7.4   Forms of communication   91
8.   Universities in focus   93
     8.1   Measuring excellence   94
     8.2   Ranking   98
9.   Research milieux *par préférence*   104
     9.1   Focal points of renewal   104
     9.2   Network milieux   112
     9.3   Characteristics of importance   117
10. Nobel laureates   129
     10.1 Nobel Prize Centennial   129
     10.2 Why Nobel laureates?   131
     10.3 Creativity on the move   135
11. Scientific careers in time and space   141
     11.1 Time-geography   141
     11.2 Life paths in the twentieth
           century   145
     11.3 Stations on a life path   148
12. Epilogue   158
     12.1 What is creativity and who is
           creative?   159
     12.2 Where does creativity appear?   161
     12.3 Why big cities?   163
     12.4 Can creativity and productivity
           be reconciled?   165

12.5 What is so different about
      successful scientific milieux?   168
12.6 What can we learn from the
      biographies of Nobel laureates?   173
12.7 Can the settings of creativity be
      designed?   176
12.8 Dichotomies of creativity   178

Notes   183
References   195
Index   209

Figures

1.1	Four Ps of creativity	3
2.1	Bisociation: Collision between association paths from two different matrices	8
6.1	Hierarchical and egalitarian organizational forms	65
6.2	Stable and unstable phases of development	74
9.1	Solitary stars and scientific networks	113
10.1	Nobel laureates in physics, chemistry and medicine, 1901–2000 (citizenship)	135
10.2	Nobel laureates in physics, chemistry and medicine, 1901–2000 (birthplace)	136
11.1	Basic concepts of time-geography	143
11.2	Life paths for a stationary and mobile person	143
11.3	Life paths of five Nobel laureates in physics	146
11.4	Settings (stations) where life paths form clusters	149
11.5	Department of Economics at the University of Chicago	150
12.1	Pairs of opposites and contrasts that generate dynamic force fields	179

Tables

8.1	Academic ranking of world universities	99
8.2	*Times Higher Education* QS World University Rankings	100
8.3	Academic ranking of world universities, 2010	102
9.1	Production and participants in networks over time	115
10.1	Nobel laureates through 2008, broken down by university	137

Preface

Once upon a time 'creativity' was seen as something divine, a gift from heaven. For a long time, skills associated with creativity were consigned to the realms of philosophy and art; nowadays they are regarded as a key source of productivity that pervades the expanding knowledge-based economy. Access to creative people is just as important for many modern firms as coal and iron once were for the steel industry. The aura and prestige surrounding scientists are brighter than ever before. Today, creativity is a topic seizing everyone's attention.

Research on creativity and innovative processes has grown immensely since World War Two.

Different approaches have been pursued, depending on the specialties and fields of research involved. Today, these are found in a lot of disciplines including humanities, social sciences, natural sciences and medicine. As a geographer, my interest was from the beginning focused on the environment – areas and places known for remarkable renewal in philosophy, mathematics, art, music, literature, technology and sciences. Soon I experienced that my own opening approach was not fruitful enough – I had to widen the scope.

Up to now, my research findings have mostly been presented in Swedish. Only shorter articles have been available in English and French. This book represents an attempt to break down a linguistic barrier, and bring work formerly hidden on a domestic shelf into a larger, international arena.

Instead of producing a long list of names, I express my sincere thanks to colleagues and graduate students in Sweden who have contributed to my research during seminars and discussions. Two individuals in particular have been helpful in bringing the project to fruition. Ken Shubert has played a crucial role in the process translating my manuscript. Sir Peter Hall, University College London, has given me generous support and inspiration. I owe a debt of gratitude to them both. Finally, *Stiftelsen Riksbankens Jubileumsfond* (The Bank of Sweden Tercentenary Foundation) triggered the whole process with generous grants, for which I am very grateful.

Gunnar Törnqvist,
Lund,
December 2011

1. Prologue

Creativity made the world we live in. If everything *not* produced by the creative mind was taken away, we would find ourselves standing naked in a primeval forest. Every culture and civilization is defined by the creative heritage passed down to it.[1]

1.1 Creativity

'Creativity' is a popular word these days. *'Créativité'* did not appear in Francophone countries until after World War Two.[2] The same is true of other languages. The English word, 'creativity' was very rarely used before the war. According to *The Oxford English Dictionary*, it made its first appearance in an 1875 book about dramatic literature, in reference to Shakespeare. Alfred North Whitehead used the word in the 1920s speaking of God.[3] Older texts relied on words such as 'imagination', 'invention', 'discovery' and 'genius' instead.

The use of the word 'creativity' has grown exponentially. A Google search generates almost half a billion hits for 'creativity' and 'creative'. Research on various types of creativity has blossomed. What lies behind these changes? Two interpretations, which are complementary rather than mutually exclusive, come to mind.

The more frequent use of the word 'creativity' is linked to general social and economic transformation. Skills that we now associate with creativity were once consigned to the realms of philosophy and art. Innovative ability is nowadays regarded as a key source of productivity that pervades the expanding knowledge-based economy and requires marketable new skills. 'Creativity' has become a fashionable word, charged with positive overtones. This can also be said about 'innovative' and 'innovation'. These observations suggest that such words and concepts are not always straightforward and unambiguous. This book will closely examine how these words are used.

'Creativity' can be defined in many different ways, depending on the context. The word derives from the Latin verb *creare*. Most scholars assume that the result of a creative process must be new and noteworthy. The next question is what constitutes newness in this sense. A common criterion is that the result of a creative process must be groundbreaking for an entire field of research or art. Furthermore, it should have long-term implications for social development. Such criteria assign creativity to an elite corps of well-known scientists, inventors and artists. Objections have been raised to this approach. Individuals can create something that is totally new for them, unaware that others have been there before. This book will later return to the question of creativity as a concept, along with its scope and deeper significance.

1.2 Points of departure

Nina Burton states that:

> Creativity is a slippery concept. While reflecting the ideals of different epochs and cultures, it is applicable to a wide range of areas and disciplines. Studies of literature, art, science and aesthetics focus on the products of creativity. Psychology looks at creative people and processes. Sociology and the humanities are interested in creative settings. Any attempt to forge a uniform definition from so many different perspectives is doomed to fail.[4]

The extensive literature about creativity and creative processes encompasses various perspectives. Figure 1.1 offers one way of classifying different points of departure. This sorting principle has appeared in the literature so often since the 1950s, that it is impossible to identify the original source.[5] The diagram is based on the four Ps of

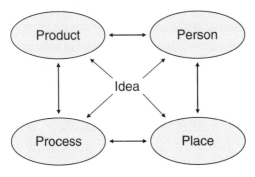

Figure 1.1   Four Ps of creativity

research on creativity: product, person, process and place. The definitions of each P are:

1. 'Product' refers to novelties in art, architecture, literature, music, philosophy, science, engineering, technology and other fields.
2. 'Person' is probably the most common point of departure. Geniuses and highly creative people have always attracted attention. Creativity among different age groups and professions, between women and men, and among more ordinary personalities, has also been studied. Furthermore, extensive literature has been devoted to helping people cultivate their own creative abilities.
3. Various branches of psychology have conducted in-depth studies of the 'process' that precedes the solution of a problem, an innovation or a new form of artistic expression. Philosophy, pedagogy and other disciplines are often fertile grounds for insights into the creative process. The reports that have been published include both basic research and applied studies.
4. 'Place' refers to the setting in which creative people work or creative processes arise. The great majority of examples in the literature come from previous epochs. It is often difficult to tell whether a current milieu will turn out to be an incubator of innovation. A place or setting may be a region, a city or an urban district. Some studies have shown that

a more profound understanding of the role of setting is unattainable until the concept is limited to smaller social systems, such as divisions within individual firms, universities and research institutions. Informal groups and networks are of particular interest. They have always been common in culture and art. Processes of scientific innovation frequently rely on collaboration among researchers from varying institutional environments.[6]

The points of departure in Figure 1.1 are not autonomous, but linked in a number of ways. People become known for what they create in music, art, literature, engineering, technology, science or another field. A successful creative process yields a result, and people are the animating force. People, processes and products may sometimes be linked to a specific place – a city, workplace or collective. This has often been the case throughout history. But today, different places commonly interact with each other.

Philosophers argue that concepts and ideas represent the fundamental expression of creative ability. Thus, the four Ps of the diagram stand for creativity in an indirect sense only. A new product is based on one or more new ideas. One or several creative persons formulate the concepts and communicate new ideas. Psychologists and other researchers have analysed the mental processes involved.[7]

This book cannot fully treat all four points of

departure identified by Figure 1.1. The expertise and perspective that such a task would require are scattered among many different disciplines. Following an overview of the literature on process, person and product, the book will turn to the places that spawn creativity and innovation.

2. Process

Psychologist J.P. Guilford introduced the concepts of 'convergent' and 'divergent' thinking in the 1950s and 1960s. Convergent thinking involves the attempt to solve problems in a traditional manner, whereas divergent thinking finds unconventional approaches. Old patterns of association and thought break down during a creative act or process. Highly creative people literally tear down walls and flee conceptual prisons and frameworks. Such a perspective on the creative is scattered throughout the literature.[1]

2.1 Bisociation

Arthur Koestler's monumental work *The Act of Creation*[2] calls attention to parallels between humour, invention and artistic creativity. His book examines different types of humour and offers many examples of authors, psychologists and philosophers who have pointed out special qualities in amusing anecdotes, which can raise hearty laughter. Koestler ascribes the following joke to Sigmund Freud:

> Two shady businessmen have succeeded in making a fortune and were trying to elbow their way into society. They had their portraits painted by a fashionable artist;

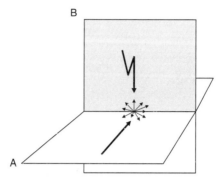

Figure 2.1   Bisociation: Collision between association paths from two different matrices

framed in gold, these were shown at a reception in the grand style. Among the guests was a well-known art critic. The beaming hosts led him to the wall on which the portraits were hanging side by side. The critic looked at them for a long time, then shook his head as if he was missing something. At length he pointed to the bare space between the pictures and asked: 'And where is the Saviour?'[3]

According to Koestler, the comic effect of a joke arises from the unexpected collision of two independent association paths. He thus introduced the concept of 'bisociation'. His exposition relies on a type of 'intellectual geometry'. Figure 2.1 represents a loose interpretation of Koestler's approach, based on the diagrams in his book. The figure shows two intersecting planes (A and B). Koestler refers to the planes as matrices that contain separate codes and regulatory systems. When the matrices intersect, a bisociative shock effect is produced. For example, in Freud's joke, the story of two ambitious businessmen who collide with the passion narrative in the New Testament.

Koestler examines the central features of a creative act by reviewing groundbreaking historical discoveries and innovations. Below are discussions of two of them: one ascribed to the mathematician Archimedes (287–212 BC) and the other to Johannes Gutenberg (1400–68).

Hieron II, king of Syracuse, was Archimedes' patron and protector. Hieron ordered Archimedes to calculate the content of gold in his crown. He wanted to make sure that the goldsmith had not added any silver. The trick was to perform the calculation without damaging the crown in any way. Archimedes knew the specific weight of gold. The problem was to determine the size of the crown. A cube, cylinder, sphere or other regular solid would not have presented any difficulty. But what was he to do about a crown studded with ornaments and filigree work? Imagine that he applied his extensive knowledge of geometry through a mental process illustrated by the arrow in matrix A of Figure 2.1.

Archimedes was in a bathtub one day when it occurred to him that the volume of the submerged part of his body must be equal to that of the water it had displaced. The problem was solved. As tradition would have it, Archimedes was so exhilarated that he jumped out of the bathtub, forgot to put his tunic and sandals back on, and ran home naked shouting 'Eureka!' ('I have found it!'). The discovery led to Archimedes' principle, according to which the buoyant force on a submerged object is equal to the weight of the fluid displaced.[4]

This story of Archimedes can be interpreted according to Figure 2.1. The theorems and rules of geometry as developed in matrix A collide with the properties of fluids as developed in matrix B. The collision, and thereby the fundamental discovery, occurs in the junction between the two matrices.

Until the early sixteenth century, books were produced by rubbing sheets of paper (or other materials), page by page, against carved or whittled blocks of wood. The rubbing process was highly time-consuming and book production was thus extremely limited. Gutenberg wrestled for many years with the problem of finding a more flexible approach. Of particular interest to him was the idea of reproducing and disseminating the Bible. He experimented with techniques used to emboss or stamp coins and seals without making any significant advances (see matrix A in Figure 2.1). One of his letters describes the flash of inspiration that broke the logjam:

> I took part in the wine harvest. I watched the wine flowing, and going back from the effect to the cause, I studied the power of this press which nothing can resist. [. . .] God has revealed to me the secret that I demanded of Him. [. . .] I have had a large quantity of lead brought to my house and that is the pen with which I shall write. [. . .] One must strike, cast, make a form like the seal of

your community; a mould such as that used for casting your pewter cups; letters in relief like those on your coins, and the punch for producing them like the foot when it multiplies its print. There is the Bible!

Gutenberg took advantage of his technical skills to make the process of printing more efficient. But the knowledge available in the area with which he was most familiar did not suffice. Not until he was confronted with the ancient technique of extracting juice from grapes did he have a stroke of genius. Molten lead could be shaped into letters and combined to form words. The printing press thus replaced rubbing, making it possible to duplicate a single page – a rapid and efficient method at the time. 'The ray of light' was the bisociation of wine press and seal – which, added together, became the letterpress.[5]

The above stories may give the impression that major discoveries and inventions are the products of luck or coincidence. But that is rarely the case. Generally speaking, skilled specialists are in a position to understand the significance of an everyday experience only after having devoted a great deal of thought to a problem and performed many experiments. For example, Archimedes wasn't the first person to step into a bathtub, but he had the requisite knowledge and insight to discover a scientific principle when observing how the water was displaced. Many people have seen apples fall from trees, but Isaac Newton was the first to associate the phenomenon with a force that could be stated as a law of motion. Every autumn, people throughout Europe witnessed the mechanical extraction of juice from grapes, but Gutenberg incorporated his observations into a method of melting lead that could be formed into letters, thereby revolutionizing the printing process.

What characterizes highly creative people is their ability to reflect on a problem for a long time in order to frame a question that opens the door to a revelation when witnessing an ordinary event. Creative people with lively imaginations have an extraordinary talent for seeing and making use of analogies between very different phenomena.

2.2   Lateral and vertical thinking

A number of books by psychologist Edward de Bono employ concepts of lateral and vertical thinking, which resemble the terminology of Guilford and Koestler. De Bono's books deal with ways that people can improve their ability to arrange information in order to solve problems and generate new ideas. He distances himself from the concept of creativity linked to artistic ability – as well as groundbreaking discoveries and inventions – focusing more on the skills required in everyday life. De Bono's argument may be summarized as follows.[6]

The brain sorts through the enormous flow of information it receives to identify patterns that enable more efficient processing. Fundamental to de Bono's thinking is that these patterns are largely shaped by the order in which the information is received and processed. A pattern tends to crystallize over time and exert a growing influence on perception. While people can easily complete existing patterns, it is difficult to change established ones in a radical way.

Patterns are an efficient way of processing information. Once the main contours of a pattern have been established, it serves as a kind of code. The advantage of such a system is that new information does not need to be comprehensive. Fragmentary data incorporated into an existing pattern can generate an overview. The problem is that such patterns and codes pose obstacles to combining bits and pieces of information in the new ways required to make major breakthroughs.

Education has always emphasized rules and logical thinking. Step-by-step learning proceeds in a predetermined direction (vertical thinking). Researchers have viewed creativity as a mysterious ability that can be fostered but not taught. Psychological studies have found that the spontaneous creativity of children often declines after a couple of years in school.

According to de Bono, creativity requires the restructuring of ingrained patterns. The ability, whether innate or developed, to transcend the limitations of previous patterns is integral to that process. Lateral thinking is needed, the fundamental principle of which is that any particular point of view is but one of many possibilities. There are just as many descriptions of a phenomenon as there are perspectives. Lateral thinking seeks alternative patterns instead of simply building on existing models.

Vertical thinking is an incremental process, whereas lateral thinking permits quantum leaps. The individual steps involved in lateral thinking need not be correct as long as the ultimate conclusion solves the problem. Instead of constantly evaluating and accepting that which appears to be correct at the moment, an assessment is postponed. Once a certain point has been reached, it is often possible to retrace a logical path to the starting point. Once that has been accomplished, the direction and order of the various steps are unlikely to matter very much. Lateral thinking is like building a vault or a bridge with scaffolding that is torn down once construction has been completed. The various parts of the bridge do not have to stand on their own during each phase of the project. But once the keystone has been laid, the entire structure must be self-supporting.

2.3   Phases of a process

In 1926, a political scientist called Graham Wallas presented what was later referred to as a model of the creative process, inspired by French mathematician Henri Poincaré (1854–1912) and his description of how he solved problems. Wallas's book was entitled *The Art of Thought*. According to the model, a creative process can be broken down into four phases:[7]

1. Preparation:
   During this phase, researchers take advantage of their knowledge and experience to identify the questions and problems that need to be addressed. The process may last for a considerable period of time, during which reflection and speculation are the order of the day.
2. Incubation:
   During this phase, questions and problems are relegated to the back burner, requiring less concentration and awareness. Relaxation and distraction promote the creative process. The brain can mull over questions and identify solutions even during sleep. Koestler maintains that bisociation and divergent thinking operate through dreams as an interaction between the conscious and unconscious minds.[8]
3. Illumination:
   This phase represents the endpoint of the creative process. A discovery or innovation can be presented to others. Research has taken a step forward. New art, music or literature has seen the light of day.
4. Verification:
   Each new result must be tested. The pioneering artist or scientist might perform such a review and decide that the creative process must start over from the beginning. Other

researchers may reject the finding, either immediately or much later. Re-evaluations and new discoveries are key catalysts of ongoing scientific progress.

3. Person

Who is creative? There are many answers to this question, which can be placed on a scale between two poles. At one pole is the idea that almost everyone has creative abilities. At the other pole is the view that only a few people are genuinely creative. Clarification of the differences between creativity and qualities such as efficiency, productivity, skill and intelligence is needed before the question can be properly addressed.

3.1 The creative child

If creativity refers to the ability to solve problems, including those that arise in everyday life, everyone has such abilities. Furthermore, practice and training can lead to improvement. But if imagination, fantasy, flexibility and originality are seen as essential to solving problems, psychological interviews, tests and experiments have demonstrated that the number of people who qualify quickly declines. Methods have been designed that permit basic types of creativity to be measured and quantified.[1]

Creativity is based on innate genetic characteristics that are moulded early in life, perhaps starting in the womb. The preschool years are important to the development of creativity. *Homo ludens* is the Latin term for 'man the player' (the child). Some people may maintain that playfulness throughout life. Studies have shown that children often exhibit creative abilities before starting school. Creativity frequently peaks at the age of six. Playfulness and imagination then often wane. Creativity spurts again in the prepubescent years.[2] Childrearing and the education system stress rules and logical thinking (see Section 2.2). Patterns and codes learned in school facilitate efficient processing of new information but may stand in the way of new thinking, as well as imaginative, childlike solutions to problems.

3.2   The creative class

Somewhere along the scale from ordinary ingenuity to genius is a definition of creativity advocated by regional economist Richard Florida in *The Rise of the Creative Class* (2001). According to Florida, a creative class has grown by leaps and bounds in the United States. In 2000, it included more than 38 million people, approximately 30 per cent of the working population. The figure was less than 10 per cent in 1900, 15 per cent in 1945 and 20 per cent in 1980. Many economically advanced countries in Europe would show similar results.

The creative American class includes a supercreative core of approximately 15 million scientists, engineers, architects, designers, educators, writers, artists, musicians and entertainers. A larger group of approximately 23 million people are business, financial, legal and healthcare professionals.[3]

The creative class according to Florida's definition comprises essentially all professions that require a long, formal education, along with various types of writers and artists. Such activities are typical of the big cities and demand qualities that are often referred to as 'human capital'. Florida's figures are reminiscent of data used to describe the contemporary economy and labour market. The expansion of formal education is an indicator of the growing knowledge-based economy. Almost half the population of many post-industrial countries obtain post-secondary (in some parts of Europe post-gymnasium) education, as opposed to less than 1 per cent just after World War Two. Wholly consistent with Florida's assertions is the fact that successful enterprises and innovative projects, such as specialized services and cultural offerings, tend to cluster in specific places, much more than they did in traditional industrial society. Florida's observations and assertions are not new. That his work is so widely discussed may be due to the title of his book. The word 'creativity' is surrounded by an aura that attracts enormous attention.

Florida's concept of creativity may be too broad. Gudmund Smith, Professor of Psychology at Lund University, writes: 'Creativity has become

a slogan. Many professions call themselves creative. But not even all artists, authors or television
producers are truly creative. Many of them are
skilful hacks or imitators.'[4]

3.3   The original creator

Psychologists and philosophers use the concept
of creativity in a very narrow sense. They warn
against confusing creativity with intelligence.
Logical, intelligent people may turn out to lack
imagination. Researchers also argue that creativity
and productivity can be mistaken for each other.
While productive people bequeath many works
to the world, a truly original creator is much less
likely to do so. It is easier to count publications
than to trace the origins of scientific inventions
and discovery. As Nils-Eric Sahlin, Professor of
Philosophy at Lund University, writes (in free
translation from Swedish):

> Mozart has great musical appeal. But how creative
> was he? He exhibited clear repetitive and receptive
> qualities. As far as I know, he was hardly a musical
> pioneer – he tore down no walls. He was a productive
> problem-solver who carried on a tradition with a sense
> of elegance, genius and precision. Anybody who had
> composed 626 works by the age of 34 must have relied
> on his predecessors. Productivity and creativity can be
> easily confused.
>
> Freud, Popper and Wittgenstein all possessed a fabu-
> lous ability to explore the recesses of philosophical and
> psychological history and find artefacts to which they
> assigned labels, quickly forgetting the names of the
> rightful owners.

Bach, Freud, Mozart, Popper, Wittgenstein and others raise an important question. Whose names are etched in the tablets of history? The names of those who are creative in a radical way, or the names of those who are productive? Those who actually invent something new, or those who borrow, adapt and modify?[5]

In the rear-view mirror of history, it is tempting to maintain that renown is always based on genuine creativity.[6] There is a tendency to mythologize great artists, inventors and scientists. Extensive case studies are required to pierce the myths and determine whether inventions and discoveries reflect true creativity and unconventional problem-solving abilities. American psychologist Robert Weisberg provided persuasive evidence of such assertions in *Beyond the Myth of Genius.* Groundbreaking scientific discoveries do not always stem from strokes of genius. Hard, persistent work that is firmly rooted in well-known theories and conventional methods often leads to the most enduring results.[7]

The above considerations make it clear that identifying original and radical creators among all the historical figures who will be discussed in this book would be an impossible task. Instead, the book will discuss individuals who contributed to scientific and artistic progress in their particular fields, regardless of whether their success was primarily due to intelligence, productivity or genuine creativity. A combination of those qualities was certainly at work in many cases.

3.4   The entrepreneur

Joseph A. Schumpeter (1883–1950), a leading twentieth-century economist, devised a ground-breaking theory of the way that innovations generate cycles ('business cycles') of growth and decline. Creative destruction powers the waves of progress in a capitalist economy. Innovative processes ripple through society. The 'entrepreneur' plays a central role by combining and refining pre-existing knowledge to spawn new products and enterprises. Schumpeter distinguishes between the concepts of 'innovation' and 'invention'. Though proficient innovators, entrepreneurs are rarely groundbreaking inventors. But they turn the ideas of inventors into marketable commodities.[8]

Economic innovations include all the processes that take place from the time an invention is made until a product is ready for the market. Product innovations may involve completely new goods or variations on old ones. Process innovations promote faster, cheaper production based on new equipment or principles of organization.

The concept of economic innovation does not stop with the production of goods. It is just as applicable to new types of services, distribution methods and administrative procedures among both private and public enterprises. The impact of institutional factors on innovative processes has been in the spotlight for a number of years. Isolated businesses are rarely innovative.

Most firms renew their production processes and develop new products and services by interacting with customers, competitors and suppliers of input goods and services. Laws, regulations and shifting patterns of culture form the framework of such collaboration. Innovative processes may take time to emerge from this web of relationships and be difficult to follow in detail. Research findings and discoveries become commercial products through a process of evolution rather than revolution.

The role of entrepreneurs is not limited to economic and business activities. Their efforts are also integral to innovation in art, music, literature, architecture, engineering, technology and science. Many prominent figures in these fields have been skilled entrepreneurs rather than groundbreaking creators, or have been able to combine qualities of both in a singular way. Some researchers are extroverted and highly visible, while others are introverted and unassuming.

Researchers are scattered at various points between two poles. At one pole are those with the ability to identify ideas and concepts whose time has come. They possess the skills required to track down suitable references in the literature. They know how to get their work published in peer-reviewed journals and anthologies. They travel a good deal, show up at conferences, present papers and cultivate an extensive network of contacts. They are able to organize, solve practical problems, obtain grants and surround themselves with competent colleagues and hard-working students. This description of the 'academic entrepreneur' is somewhat of a caricature.

At the other pole are 'pioneers' – eccentric, imaginative, visionary, original, talented and bursting with ideas. They may have difficulty communicating with others and standing up for themselves. Their forward-looking attitude and quest for new approaches may cause them to be misunderstood and neglected by their colleagues, or to be regarded as oddballs. They frequently have trouble obtaining research grants. The originality and importance of their ideas may not be fully appreciated until long afterwards.

It is easier to earmark resources for entrepreneurs than pioneers. There are many entrepreneurs, and the results of their work are visible and relatively easy to quantify. Pioneers are few in number, and the significance of their discoveries cannot be evaluated right away. Moreover, their efforts involve risk-taking and constant setbacks. More often than not, they find themselves on the edge. A successful research setting must make room for both entrepreneurs and pioneers. They complement each other and set the stage for efficiency and productivity, as well as the kind of genuine creativity on which innovation and development rest. Research is inevitably something of an elitist project, characterized by risk-taking and uncertainty.[9]

4. Place

Can a place or setting be creative? Not in a literal sense, any more than a place can be happy, exhilarated, curious or angry. The term 'creative milieu' presupposes that the people who live and work there, along with their thoughts and ideas, possess such qualities. Individuals, working both independently and collaboratively, make the discoveries and inventions for which a place becomes known. A place is an arena in which creative processes can unfold. Of particular relevance is whether a particular setting stimulates or obstructs creativity and entrepreneurship. A key challenge is to identify the characteristics of a place that either attract or repel pioneers and entrepreneurs.

4.1   The concept of place

The painter at her easel, the composer at her piano, the author at her desk or the researcher in her laboratory or at a computer all symbolize creative acts that take place in a private setting. At least during some phases of a creative process, privacy is essential to the kind of concentration that acts of creativity require. But only in rare cases does groundbreaking renewal stem from individual creativity. Usually it is the product of a collective effort. Ideas bubble forth from a repository of experience acquired in interaction with one's surroundings. Innovative processes cannot survive very long without external stimuli.

The concept of place refers to environments in which creators and entrepreneurs – whether scientists or artists – work and their innovative abilities come to light. A fundamental assumption, strongly supported by the literature, is that creative processes make similar demands on settings and their characteristics regardless of the discipline involved.

Regions and districts with their built-up areas, facilities, institutions and inhabitants are examples of large-scale settings. Cities and towns are textbook cases of smaller settings, easier to analyse in detail. Organizations, institutions, firms and workplaces are closer to the core of the creative process. Studies of informal social groups and private contact networks permit even greater insight.

This chapter is devoted to various urban milieux throughout history. The discussion is limited to the West, primarily Europe. While desirable, an overview of global conditions is outside the scope of this book. The material is largely based on extracts and summaries of previously published texts.[1]

4.2   Ancient and Renaissance cities

The first object of study is Athens, arguably the cradle of Western culture, though deeply indebted to older Asian civilizations. Athens's heyday was the fifth century BC. Descriptions of ancient settings are fragmentary, based on ruins, damaged sculptures and scraps of manuscripts. Much of the knowledge was handed down by oral tradition.

Athens was a very big city for its time. Somewhere between 300,000 and 500,000 people lived near the Acropolis and in the surrounding countryside. Forty thousand of them were citizens with political influence, while 200,000 were women and children, and 100,000 were slaves. The Greek word *agora* means not only a market and meeting place but also a crowd of people, a meaning worth noticing. The Agora was located below the Acropolis. Ideas and conversation were fundamental to life in Athens. Most people lived in slum-like conditions already before the erections of the architectural creations we see the ruins of today.

This milieu has often been regarded as a centre of renewal in philosophy, theatre, music, politics, art and architecture. Protagoras, Socrates, Plato and Aristotle are legendary philosophers. Aeschylus, Sophocles and Euripides are among the great Western dramatists. Institutions of higher education were the cultural breeding grounds of the time. Plato founded the Academy and Aristotle started the Lyceum. Gymnasiums were public institutions for physical education. Some of them had lecture halls in which philosophers and rhetoricians performed.

Much of the innovation ascribed to ancient

Greece occurred not in Athens, but in smaller city-states on the islands and coast of the Mediterranean. Coins and the alphabet were developed in Ionia on the west coast of Asia Minor. Democritus of Macedonia postulated the first atomic theory. Pythagoras and the Pythagoreans of Sicily created a mathematical structure for ancient thought.

Greater Greece of the fifth century BC comprised approximately 1,500 city-states – trading stations and development centres linked by culture, navigation routes and a common language. The system of cities and trading areas supported a remarkably high standard of living for the political and economic elite, if not for the general population. Economic surplus was a precondition of the flowering of culture.

The conquests of Alexander the Great in Asia and Northern Africa considerably expanded the intellectual scope of ancient Greece. Hellenism arose from the cross-pollination of different cultures. *Hellas* was the Greek word for Greece. Mathematics, physics, astronomy and geography became independent disciplines. Archimedes of Sicily (287–212 BC) was a leading mathematician and physicist. A scientific centre emerged in Alexandria, a planned city founded by Alexander the Great, west of the mouth of the Nile. Geographers Eratosthenes and Ptolemy were among the city's many scientists. Their contributions to our view of the Earth included poles, an equator, an ecliptic, tropical circles and meridians.

Eratosthenes (276–195 BC), a grammarian and poet as well as a geographer, calculated the circumference of the Earth with great precision on the basis of theoretical considerations. He then proceeded to measure the altitude of the sun in Alexandria and Syene directly to the south, basing his calculations on the distance between them. In the third century BC, Aristarchos of Samos maintained that the Earth rotated on its axis and revolved around the Sun. He was accused of having disturbed the peace of the gods.

The Museion, a library of unprecedented size, was built in Alexandria around 300 BC. The library housed some 400,000 papyrus scrolls, a complete compilation of Hellenic culture. It was also a meeting place for leading philosophers and scientists. Christian fanatics burned the Museion down in the fifth century AD. Some of the texts were reconstructed much later from Arabic sources.

A question may conclude this review of the ancients. What would have happened if Columbus had known about Eratosthenes' calculation of the Earth's circumference? He might have realized where he was when he reached the Bahamas, Cuba and Haiti on his way to India in 1492.

Florence typifies the urban culture that emerged and the cultural revival that took place in Europe during the late Middle Ages and Renaissance. Lasting from approximately 1350 to 1550, the

Renaissance marked the rebirth of interest in the ancient art and world of ideas of which Athens and Rome were centres.

Princes and other rulers founded hundreds of European cities in the thirteenth and fourteenth centuries. Some cities of antiquity were resurrected in Southern Europe. Among the factors that contributed to the growth of the cities were expanding populations and improved transportation. Majestic cathedrals were built and universities were established, starting in Bologna in 1088, followed by Padua, Florence and Pisa. Northern Italy boasted of more than a dozen universities in the fifteenth century. As in ancient Greece, city-states of various sizes were the dominant economic and political forces throughout much of Europe.

A Platonic academy was founded in Florence, and a labour market was created for learned humanists in philosophy, literature and history. But the Florentine setting was most innovative when it came to art and architecture. A new school of art added both depth and perspective to Renaissance painting. Paulo Uccello was a leading painter, while Giotto di Bondone and Filippo Brunelleschi were architects as well. They collaborated with mathematicians to develop the concept of central perspective. Among other Florentine artists were Michelangelo Buonarotti and Raffaello Santi, known as Rafael. Leonardo da Vinci, who spent some time in the city, was not limited to painting, drawing and sculpture. He was also a leading scientist, mathematician, musician and engineer. His catapults, tanks, flying machines and parachutes were far ahead of their time.

While all of the above scientists and artists spent time in Florence, most of them also worked in other places. As pioneers and entrepreneurs, they moved around in search of new models, sources of inspiration and milieu that could provide a livelihood and favourable working conditions.

Florence was a city of contrasts and contradictions. The city-states of Northern Italy were often at war with each other. Foreign armies were a common threat, forcing the rural population to seek refuge inside the walls of the city. Plagues and famines significantly reduced the size of the population. What was special about Florence, as well as Venice in many respects, was its economy.

An extensive textile industry and various types of handicrafts sprung up in Florence. The city became a trading centre at a time when roads crossed the Arno River as far upstream as the river was navigable. A monetary economy emerged and Florence became a European banking centre. Merchants formed large trading monopolies in various sectors. The Medici family came to power in the fifteenth century after having acquired a gigantic fortune through banking operations that branched out to many parts of Europe. The concentration of capital was integral to Florence's status as a hotbed of innovation. Nobody could compete with the Medicis as patrons of the humanities, art and architecture.

4.3   The rise of modern cities

The period from 1850 to 1950 was characterized by the thoroughgoing transformation of political, economic and social conditions in Europe. World War One shook the foundations of society. Monarchies crumbled. Revolution broke out in Russia. Industrial forms of production, socialist movements, radically improved transportation and communication, and public education shaped a new world. Innovative processes abounded in engineering, science, art, architecture and literature. World War Two unleashed unprecedented destruction. Any number of cities and places can illustrate the transformational nature of the period. Below are a few that have received particular attention in the literature.

Vienna from 1880 to 1930 exhibited many of the creative processes that are relevant to this book. The Austro-Hungarian Empire collapsed, World War One ended in defeat and the Republic of Austria emerged. Composers Arnold Schoenberg and Gustav Mahler became famous in this milieu. Sigmund Freud and Carl Gustav Jung were prominent figures and precursors in psychoanalysis. Gustav Klimt and Oskar Kokoschska were among the leading artists. Architects Otto Wagner and Adolf Loos pioneered functionalism and art nouveau. Author Elias Canetti spent the seminal years of his youth in Vienna. Philosophers Otto Weininger and Ludwig Wittgenstein were active in the city at times. Author and journalist Karl

Kraus served as a central figure and communication link between many different specialists.

Well-known scientists in the Viennese setting included physicists Ludwig Boltzmann and Heinrich Hertz, as well as medical specialists Robert Bárány, Julius Wagner-Jauregg, Karl Landsteiner and Konrad Lorenz. Joseph Schumpeter, a pioneer in economics, started off in Vienna.[2]

Why so many ostensibly independent disciplines such as philosophy, the theory of science, economics, medicine, psychiatry, mathematics, poetry, music, art, architecture, theatre and journalism thoroughly transformed during the same period and in the same city is one of the questions which will be addressed in subsequent chapters.

Long a provincial town in one of many small principalities, Berlin quickly became one of Europe's biggest and most important cities following the unification of Germany in 1871. The Berlin of the 1920s competed with both London and Paris as a cultural centre and surpassed them when it came to technological development. The city was in the forefront of the various currents of Western art, music and literature collectively referred to as 'modernism'.

Berlin attracted artists and authors from Austria, the United States and Britain, not to mention intellectuals from Eastern Europe. During and after the Russian Revolution, some 360,000 members of the intelligentsia and bourgeoisie immigrated to Berlin. Eighty-six Russian publishing houses set up store there. There were a number of daily Russian newspapers. Russian bookstores opened. For several years, Berlin was referred to as the capital of Russian literature.

Many well-known artists and scientists worked in Berlin before returning to their native countries or moving on. The following discussion will focus on those associated with *Der Sturm*, a magazine of expressionism, as well as the galleries, publishers and literary salons in its sphere of interest. The bimonthly, which was founded in 1910 by Herwarth Walden, lived on until 1932.

Among the most famous writers associated with these cultural currents in Berlin were Max Brod, Franz Kafka, Anatole France, Knut Hamsun, Heinrich Mann, Karl Kraus and Selma Lagerlöf. The roster of artists included Oskar Kokoschka, Marc Chagall and Wassily Kandinsky. The district of theatres, publishing houses and cafes attracted many other cultural figures of interwar Europe. Albert Einstein was Director of Berlin's Kaiser Wilhelm Institute of Physics from 1913 to 1933. It all came to an abrupt halt when Hitler was appointed as Chancellor in 1933.[3]

Paris prospered between the wars. The city simmered with cultural vitality and artistic experimentation. It was not simply a centre for the French intellectual elite, but attracted writers, artists, sculptors, filmmakers and composers from around the world. Some 200,000 Russian aristocrats and anti-Bolsheviks fled to Paris, many through Berlin. Americans came in order to escape provincialism, racial prejudice, prohibition and middle-class values. Many of them were bohemians in the true sense of the word. Due to overcrowded housing conditions, cafes, galleries and museums were particularly popular rendezvous points. Following is the story of a bookstore that became a microcosm of the Paris scene in this whirlwind of activity.

Adrienne Monniers and Sylvia Beach, an American, opened the Shakespeare and Company bookstore on rue de l'Odéon in 1919. It subsequently moved to rue de la Bûcherie on the Left Bank, adjacent to Notre Dame Cathedral, where it remains to this day. The first group of artists and writers who found their way to the bookstore belonged to the Lost Generation, those who had fought in World War One and stayed on in Paris. Visitors, particularly from the United States, came to Shakespeare and Company later on. It served as a club for both English- and French-speaking writers, including André Gide, James Joyce, Gertrude Stein, Ezra Pound, F. Scott Fitzgerald, Henry Miller and Samuel Beckett. Jean-Paul Sartre, Simone de Beauvoir and Albert Camus lived in the same environment. Ernest Hemingway's *A Moveable Feast* describes the Parisian cultural world during that period.[4]

London from 1904 to 1956 was the home of a well-known group of intellectuals, writers and artists, in some respects reminiscent of Paris. The Bloomsbury Group was named after the area in which most of its members lived. The University of London, University College and British Museum – as well as many theatres, libraries, publishing houses and bookstores – are all in Bloomsbury. Pubs and restaurants line the streets. The list of scientists, writers and artists who have lived there at one time or another is comprehensive.

The core of the Bloomsbury Group was not particularly large but branched out in many directions. It was held together by close personal contact, liberal social values and a critique of Victorian conventions. Most of them had been associated with Cambridge and were influenced by G.E. Moore, Bertrand Russell and other philosophers. Among its most famous members were writers E.M. Forster and Virginia Woolf, artists Vanessa Bell and Duncan Grant, art critics Roger Fry and Clive Bell, and economist John Maynard Keynes.[5]

The growing industrial towns and cities may not be among the places that are spontaneously associated with creativity. But they have often served as breeding grounds of innovation. Manchester illustrates the creative processes that characterize industrial society and the fact that only a very short period of time (around 1840 in this case) may be involved. Industrialism made its definitive breakthrough in the city. A series of technological innovations transformed cotton manufacturing in the late eighteenth century. Half a century later, a number of technological changes were associated with Manchester. The city is a good example of the way that breakthroughs cluster in both time and space. Technological advances reflect institutional conditions, along with a critical mass of knowledge at a particular place and within a particular discipline. The closer the relationship between technological inventions, innovations and practical applications, the faster the social transformation and the more profound the impact on social conditions.

John Dalton, sometimes referred to as the father of modern atomic theory, was a Mancunian schoolteacher. James Prescott Joule discovered a law for the correlation between heat, amperage, resistance and time. Friedrich Engels studied the social consequences of industrialization. Richard Cobden and John Bright formulated Manchester Liberalism. Chartism, a British form of liberalism, was first articulated in the city. Experimentalism and renewal were rampant in architecture, art and music.

The physical sciences became established disciplines at nineteenth-century German universities. With many students and considerable economic resources, chemistry and physics were particularly popular topics of research at the end of the century. The disciplines were broken down into experimental and theoretical branches. The city of Göttingen, the true cradle of quantum mechanics, is a second example of the shared interests of science and industry. Manufacturing industries employed university-trained scientists as directors of research and development.

With the financial backing of Bayer, a chemical company, mathematician Felix Klein founded Institut für Physikalische Chemie und Elektrochemie, the first independent research institute at a German university, in the mid 1890s. Walther Nernst, its director, was awarded the Nobel Prize in Chemistry in 1920. Many new institutions, wholly or partially financed by industrial companies, appeared as time went by. Klein also founded Göttinger Vereinung, an association of scientists, engineers and industrialists that built bridges between science, engineering and industry. Among the well-known industrialists involved were Alfred Krupp and Werner von Siemens.

Historians have identified at least two industrial revolutions. The first one began in Britain in the late eighteenth century and was spurred on by the steam engine, mechanical loom, new metallurgical processes and other technological inventions. Machines began to replace hand tools. The second industrial revolution, which started in the mid nineteenth century, is associated with improved steel manufacture, the breakthrough of electricity, the internal combustion engine, chemicals, the telegraph and telephone. While the first revolution was based largely on advanced craftsmanship and engineering, the second relied more on what we now call scientific research.

As Spanish-American sociologist Manuel Castells has argued, the transition from agrarian to industrial society involved truly revolutionary changes. Waves of technical innovations and applications transformed production and distribution processes, generated a host of new products and decisively altered the geographic distribution of wealth and power. The ascendancy of the West, essentially limited to Britain and a handful of other European countries – as well as their North American and Australian offshoots – was fundamentally linked to the technological superiority that emerged during the two industrial revolutions.[6]

The second industrial revolution was dominated by Germany and the United States, which accounted for most progress in chemistry, electricity and telephony. An analysis by British geographers Peter Hall and Pascal Preston shows the importance of local breeding grounds in the geographic redistribution of technological innovations after the mid nineteenth century. Berlin, New York and Boston were the world's hi-tech centres from 1880 to 1914, while London was a pale semblance of Berlin.[7]

4.4 Localized features in common

European history presents celebrated examples of cities and places that have served as hothouses of creativity in art, architecture, philosophy, music, literature, science, engineering and technology. Many of the pioneers and entrepreneurs associated with these places were born and raised elsewhere. Some of them moved a number of times and cultivated their creative abilities in a number of different settings. What has made some places attractive and others not?

Capital has always attracted talented people. Patrons with financial resources to spare have supported the arts and sciences. These days, they would be referred to as 'sponsors'. They could be found in Athens and the world of Hellenistic culture around the Mediterranean. The Church and many royal houses attracted builders, artists and humanists during the Medieval and Renaissance periods. Palaces, cathedrals and universities still stand as visible reminders of places in which power was wed to money. Artists and various types of specialists have always plied their trades in large cities and towns.

What kind of cultural centre would Florence have been without its banking system, textile industry and trade, not to mention the Medici and Pitti families? With its musical life, science and art, Vienna was still the political and economic hub of a far-flung, multicultural empire in the early twentieth century. London was the centre of power and wealth in a global empire. After German unification in 1871, Berlin quickly became a continental metropolis. During different eras, Paris has been Europe's cultural centre, attracting intellectuals and artists from around the world. The technical innovations of industrialism set the stage for mass production and the geographic redistribution of capital. Manchester, Göttingen, London, Berlin, New York, Boston and other cities took turns as hubs of technological progress and industrial development.

Cities have always offered meeting places where people could get together on a formal or informal basis. They were particularly important when conversation and direct personal contact were basically the only ways to convey information. Given modern means of transportation and communication, their current role is more surprising and will require a more detailed discussion in a subsequent chapter.

The agora, forum and piazza served as public meeting places in antiquity, the Middle Ages and Renaissance, respectively. People travelled on foot through the crowded city centres. The Mediterranean climate allowed them to meet outdoors for much of the year. Indoor facilities were needed farther north. The cafes of *fin de siècle* Vienna are legendary. Rapid population growth had spawned housing shortages. In addition to private society, prominent intellectuals and artists fraternized and conversed at cafes. Both general ideas and detailed technical information circulated in close-knit networks. Specialists unabashedly crossed boundaries to other professional domains.

London, Berlin and Paris featured many cafes and restaurants. Berlin had a magazine, as well as publishing houses, art galleries, theatres and literary salons, where writers and artists could meet. A Parisian bookstore was a prominent gathering place, publisher and post office for artists, writers, bohemians and political refugees. The chamber of commerce and workers' organizations of Manchester offered premises to both capitalists and the proletariat. In other parts of the world, churches, chapels and clubs were important gathering spots.

The geographic settings presented as breeding grounds for creative processes have not only served as meeting places for local residents. They have also been key focal points for travellers, and – as cosmopolitan metropolises – facilitated communication and information sharing with the outside world. With its port of Piraeus, Athens was the central trading station around the Mediterranean. Florence grew in its capacity as a hub of river and overland transportation. Vienna became a crossroads where shipping between the East and West on the Danube intersected with North–South trading on the plains east of the Alps. The Romans exploited the strategic positions of Paris and London as junctions between overland and sea transportation. When railway construction began, Manchester and Berlin emerged as central nodes in the networks of expanding industrialism.

One of the works by contemporary Swedish playwright Lars Norén is entitled *Kaos är granne med Gud* (*Chaos is a Neighbour of God*). Taken from a poem by Erik Johan Stagnelius (1793–1823), the title suggests that chaotic circumstances provide fertile soil for creativity and innovation. Diversity and variation – as opposed to uniformity, similarity and homogeneity – favour creative processes. Many examples in the literature suggest that creative settings have often bordered on chaos. Creative processes and thoroughgoing innovation have generally begun when unique abilities and close communication coincided with instability and uncertainty. All creative processes – whether technological inventions, groundbreaking research or new schools of art – have taken systematic advantage of structural instability, to one extent or another.[8]

Structural instability makes it easier for a pioneer to break with ingrained patterns of thought and rigid regulations (see the concepts of divergent and lateral thinking as discussed in Chapter 2). Stable periods, as well as carefully regulated and planned settings, have rarely been creative in the deeper sense of the word. Wars and revolutions have given rise to inventions and transformational changes. The French Revolution, and the Russian Revolution to a lesser extent, led to innovation and new ways of thinking largely unrelated to ideology, politics or forms of government. The rapid expansion of Western economies in the 1950s and 1960s stemmed partly from creative processes generated by World War Two.

Fin de siècle Vienna was a chaotic setting in which many people suffered. The Austro-Hungarian Empire collapsed, World War One ended in defeat, and civil war raged. A semi-totalitarian regime and rigid upper-middle-class values had stood in the way of social, political, economic and cultural experimentation. All such inhibitions were swept away by the war. Pent-up energy gushed forth. Old authoritarian structures were abolished, a republican form of government was adopted and outworn institutions dissolved, replaced initially by ad hoc, informal, institutional creations and experimentation. Diverse ideas and styles blossomed all at once. In the parlance of the time, Viennese culture had been 'Balkanized'. Berlin exhibited clear parallels during the period. Following defeat in the war, revolution and the collapse of the empire in 1918, its political and cultural life was just as chaotic as that of Vienna.

Manchester was also chaotic in 1840. Society lacked physical and social organization. Though big for its time, the city had little formal government. The education system was characterized by diversity and variation. Abrupt, unplanned and unstructured change typified the intellectual milieu. Manchester of the 1840s has been compared to Silicon Valley of the 1950s. Interwar Paris, revolutionary St Petersburg, the Bloomsbury area of London, and the Los Alamos National Laboratory base in the United States, which opened in 1943, exhibited clear signs of institutional incoherence and social disorganization.

Even scientists in well-planned research parks and development centres do not, as a rule, get beyond preparations for the actual process. The requisite components are concentrated in a small area. That which subsequently occurs is very difficult to observe. Outsiders are left with a chaotic impression. Interesting events sometimes occur in this artificial environment. But synergies are rare. In other words, the final results are no greater than the sum of the partial results that each unit would have generated, even in the absence of extraordinary measures and the construction of centres.

However, there is no unambiguous correlation between chaos and creativity. In speaking of chemist and Nobel laureate Ilya Prigogine, Nina Burton has argued that both life and art emerge at the intersection of chaos, organization and chance: 'Perfect order is crystalline death; total chaos is formless death. Between them is a fantastic cross-fertilisation of perspective and surprise on which creativity is based. That is the source of all potential.'[9]

We have seen how every epoch has had urban milieux that spawned renewal and development in different fields. Descriptions of these settings reveal that smaller groups and social systems of individuals – bound by common interests, proximity and a sense of affinity – have been the true breeding grounds of creativity, often serving as meeting places for cosmopolitan pioneers and entrepreneurs.

5. Metropolis

Metropolis, which comes from the Greek words for mother and city, was originally referred to as the capital of an ecclesiastical province. These days it denotes a very large city, a significant centre. The roots of the word suggest a place where new ideas are born and from where change integral to the progress of civilization starts.

Throughout history, cities have not only served as centres for the exchange of goods and services, for human collaboration and encounters, they have also received waves of immigration. They have been crucibles of alienation as well as community. Cities have been melting pots where different cultures, religions, lifestyles and political outlooks have interacted and merged. They have been the focal points of change. Most revolutions have broken out in cities. New fashions, styles and technologies have seen the light of day there. Innovations in the areas of business management, organization of labour and lifestyle have been first tried in the cities. Such changes, even those that originally emerged elsewhere, have rippled out from the cities.

Many researchers have examined the particular conditions that characterize modern cities as breeding grounds of creativity and innovation.

All of them stress characteristics of big cities that promote innovative processes while attracting entrepreneurs and creative people.

5.1 Communication and cultural diversity

Cities in Civilization by British geographer Peter Hall contains an in-depth analysis of the qualities that are peculiar to big cities. Arguing that they have reflected the cultural evolution of the West throughout history, he proceeds from several fundamental questions:

> Why do great cities have golden ages and how do they come about? Why does the creative flame burn in cities rather than the countryside? What makes a city exceptionally creative and innovative at a particular time? Why does this spirit flower for a few years, a decade or two at most, and disappear as suddenly as it arrived? Why do so few cities have more than one such golden age? What prevents them recapturing the spark that once animated them?[1]

Swedish economist Åke E. Andersson developed the concept of the rise of a knowledge-based economy in the mid 1980s. His main thesis was that such an economy is based on culture, communication and creativity. He regards each of those areas as strategically vital to contemporary social development. The dynamic that they generate is particularly evident in big cities and centres.[2]

Two fundamental concepts predominate in a knowledge-based economy. 'Physical infrastructure' refers to various types of installations and built-up areas, particularly those that facilitate transport and communication. 'Cultural infrastructure' refers to intangible phenomena such as the promotion and development of knowledge, along with various kinds of cultural events and activities. Many important characteristics of an urban environment can be classified according to these two concepts.

Charles Landry is among the recent researchers who have emphasized a combination of institutional clustering, physical infrastructure and cultural diversity in the big cities. His *The Creative City: A Toolkit for Urban Innovators* devotes a great deal of space to practical urban planning issues. He has worked for many years as a consultant in revitalizing the urban environments of more than 30 countries.[3]

One of the most obvious geographic advantages of cities is that they offer different types of proximity. Territorial proximity is synonymous with concentration and neighbourhood. Networking with other cities is another kind of proximity. Sophisticated transport and communication systems connect people, installations and built-up areas regardless of physical distance. Cities have become hubs of continental and global flows of goods, people, information and capital. Furthermore, the mass media broadcast information and entertainment from a small number of cities.

Many of the advantages offered by metropolises stem from their importance as centres of finance, power, transportation and communication. The administration and management of firms, financial institutions, research projects, trade organizations and the public sector amass in the big cities. Institutional clustering is greater than elsewhere, offering a wide range of services and job opportunities. An advanced cultural infrastructure serves as a hotbed of diversity. Large, dense urban environments provide much more in the way of cultural amenities than small ones – both in absolute terms and in relation to the size of the population.

Sweden, which has only nine million inhabitants, typifies this concentration of cultural activities. According to geographer Kerstin Cederlund, approximately 14 per cent of the population lived in Stockholm, the biggest urban region, at the beginning of the twenty-first century. The region housed more than 90 per cent of all music publishers, 75 per cent of film companies and almost 40 per cent of publishing houses. However, the publishing houses faced significant competition from Lund, Uppsala and other university towns. The region was also the home of the country's radio and television producers, as well as newspapers and magazines. It had the biggest shopping centres and theatres. A considerable majority of actors, writers, musicians, composers, artists and other cultural workers tended to live in the region.[4] International literature about the big Western metropolises describes a similar pattern.

The cultural infrastructure is larger and more concentrated in big centres and metropolises than the relative size of their populations would suggest – notable but not a surprise. The key markets for cultural activities are in the metropolises. Their cultural offerings attract not only the local population but tourists and other visitors. Big theatres, opera houses, concert halls, museums and other institutions draw people from far and wide.

The metropolises offer a robust, diverse employment market for various types of cultural workers. The market provides alternatives when particular activities dwindle or disappear. Opportunities exist to combine various sources of income. An actor or musician can move from one theatre, concert hall, film or event to another. They can appear on radio and television and thus achieve celebrity status. The metropolises have a cultural web that is bigger and more concentrated than the smaller cities. Urban regions around the world serve as escalators on which artists and intellectuals can build and advance their careers.[5]

5.2 Creative capital

Access to creative people is just as important for many modern firms as coal and iron once were for the steel industry. Richard Florida argues that theories according to which people are drawn to places that offer job opportunities are less valid than they once were. These days, people are often motivated by personal interest and lifestyle. A business that needs skilled workers must follow them. As Hewlett-Packard CEO Carley Fiorina once told the US governors: 'Keep your tax incentives and highway interchanges; we will go where the highly skilled people are.'[6]

What is so special about the places in which creative people choose to live? Florida addresses the question in *The Rise of the Creative Class*. His broad definition of the creative class includes 38 million Americans, approximately one-third of the working population. The class contains a super-creative core of researchers and engineers, professors, poets, writers, artists, actors, designers, architects, publishers, analysts and authors of technical books. Around them is a broad range of knowledge-intensive industries, including technology, finance, the judiciary, hospitals and stock exchanges.[7] Of course, pioneers can be found throughout this class and in all of these industries. But probably the great majority are rather skilful entrepreneurs, intelligent and well-educated people – talented and successful specialists of various kinds.

The places and regions that Florida considers to be attractive for such people are characterized by technology, talent and tolerance. Each of these assets is a necessary but insufficient condition. All of them must coalesce at the same time and place in order to draw creative people, generate innovation and stimulate economic growth. That is when a place becomes a creative centre.

Without presenting a closer examination of

Florida's database and statistical methods (such as the use of indexes to weight different variables), his work may be summarized as follows. The technology of a place can be assessed according to the number of patents per capita, as well as the concentration of software, electronic and biomedical production. Talent is measured by the percentage of a place's, or region's, population that belongs to the creative class. Up to this point, Florida's research is consistent with previous works that stress the clustering of technology and skills as a key prerequisite for economic development and regional growth.

Florida's focus on tolerance is often regarded as the most groundbreaking aspect of his analysis. His regional gauge of tolerance consists of several components – including the percentage of immigrants. Other studies confirm that people from abroad were integral to US economic growth in the 1990s. The number of New Yorkers born abroad rose from 28 per cent in 1989 to 40 per cent in 1999. Almost 25 per cent of the total Silicon Valley population, and more than 30 per cent of researchers and engineers, were immigrants. The biggest threat posed to ongoing progress in the United States may not be terrorism but a future where creative and talented people will be less inclined to move to the country.[8]

Florida also constructs a Bohemian index by measuring the percentage of musicians, writers, designers, actors, directors, photographers and dancers in a place or region. His 'Gay Index', the percentage of homosexuals in a population, is his most observed indicator of tolerance and diversity. A place that welcomes homosexuals is likely to be tolerant when it comes to other people as well. Faced with criticism of his argument, Florida stresses in the preface to the Swedish translation of *The Rise of the Creative Class* that the presence of homosexuals and bohemians does not literally cause a region to grow but rather serves as an indicator – a gauge of the kind of openness and cultural diversity that promotes creativity.

For many different urban regions the variables mentioned are combined in a creativity index. Among significant creative centres (regions with more than one million inhabitants) are San Francisco, Austin, San Diego, Boston, Seattle, Raleigh-Durham, Houston, Baltimore-Washington, New York and Dallas. They may be regarded as the US equivalents to the older European metropolises presented in previous chapters.

The firm is the central organizational unit in established economic literature. Firms are the units that power competition, though dependent on the regional and national setting in which they operate.[9] But Florida maintains that the primary competition these days is between places. Place is becoming the most important economic and social unit of our time and has assumed many of the functions that were previously ascribed to individual firms. Large, permanent organizations with clearly identifiable employees are being replaced by small, flexible networks that constantly change shape as the many components of a local or regional setting reassemble.

The American geographer Michael Storper gives us an illustration of this trend. Hollywood was once dominated by large studios that signed long-term contracts with actors, producers and technicians. Films were produced on an assembly line basis. When the system broke down in the 1950s, a more flexible model emerged. A producer can now sell a script idea to a group of investors and then put together a team of actors and technicians. Once the film has been completed, the team splits up and reconfigures around new ideas.[10]

Florida writes of the 'horizontal job market'. Specialists pursue horizontal rather than vertical careers. People do not stay at the same company for very long. They advance by moving vertically from company to company. Americans change jobs at an average of once every three years. Jobs or occupations are turning into 'clusters of specialised knowledge'.[11]

When a firm becomes a less significant organizational unit and is partially replaced by a temporary, project-oriented constellation, the need for external meeting places is likely to increase. Such forums once played a major role in European cities due to overcrowding before large workplaces had become the norm (see Chapter 4). American sociologist Ray Oldenburg talks of the 'third place', which facilitates informal encounters in an urban environment. The home is the first place, while the job is the second. A third place may be a cafe, bar, restaurant or other public establishment, often centrally located. Modern urban planning has increased distances such that communication and social life at home and on the job have become less feasible.[12]

Adam Smith (1723–90) stressed the role of education in an individual's productivity. Contemporary economists have constructed theories to describe how investment in education and health care boosts productivity and efficiency, and thereby the competitiveness and welfare of a nation or region. During the 1960s, Theodore W. Schultz of the University of Chicago developed the concept of 'human capital' as a vital factor of production. He was awarded the Sveriges Riksbank Prize in Economic Sciences in Memory of Alfred Nobel in 1979.[13]

Human capital refers to qualities that are fundamentally linked to individuals. 'Social capital' is related to interpersonal relations. To give a simplified picture, human capital resides in the nodes of a nodal network, and social capital in the links between them. The human capital of an area is the sum of the skills and productivity of its inhabitants. Its social capital describes the ability of a population to cooperate and interact socially. Institutional conditions play a major role in that respect.[14]

A number of works emphasize the importance of social capital. Among the best-known studies in the area of local and regional development are those by the American political scientist Robert D. Putnam, concerning Italy after the political reform of the early 1970s. The reform decentralized political power and the public sector from Rome to 20 regions. Putnam and his colleagues monitored the reform for two decades, concluding that the repercussions were significant in Northern Italy but inconsequential in the southern part of the country.[15]

In the north, the citizens became more politically involved, while public bodies and institutions grew more efficient. For Putnam, this reflects a strong civil spirit which he calls 'civility'. Very little changed in Southern Italy, which did not have a comparable tradition of civic commitment. Public life had been structured vertically rather than horizontally. Putnam sees these differences as the result of a long historical process, particularly the dominance of the Mafia and Catholic Church and their impact on values and motivation among the general population. The city-states in the northern part of the country had been open to the rest of the world in a completely different way. Trade and new ideas were welcome. Respect for individual initiative developed.

The importance of social capital is not apparent in politics only. Its economic role is just as obvious. The 'Third Italy,' a frequently cited example, encompasses the Emilia Romagna and Veneto regions of the north-eastern Italian Peninsula, including Bologna, Carpi, Sassuolo and Arezzo.[16] The area houses many small handicraft-oriented firms, frequently family-owned. There are plenty of skilled entrepreneurs and an established tradition of risk-taking. Failure is not regarded as shameful. A complex, supportive network – a social web – of private economic associations, along with political organizations, create well-functioning markets and provide small businesses with an infrastructure that they would be unable to sustain on their own.

The networks channel information about technological innovations, creditworthiness and reliability. They are created, maintained, upgraded and expanded through informal contacts in associations, clubs, cafes, bars and on street corners. An ostensibly conflicting combination of competition and collaboration arises. Similar settings are identifiable in most industrialized countries. For example, local popular movements – rooted in religious faith, political conviction or sports – have historically generated social capital in the Nordic countries.

Social capital as a concept clearly illustrates the energy that can emerge from collaboration and competition in close-knit networks. Places that have abundant social capital are characterized by trust and tradition, often synonymous with shared perspectives, inherited norms and scepticism to change. Nourished by local and regional culture, the energy paves the way for success among native entrepreneurs and small businesses. But what happens to creativity in areas with significant social capital? According to

Florida, social capital is compatible with creativity to a limited extent only. The industrial districts discussed above are not breeding grounds of radical creative processes.

Areas with social capital contain strong links between people that provide security and stability but that can also lead to social isolation, repetitiveness and stagnation. They favour people who belong to the in-group but penalize those who do not. Strong links are not fertile grounds for creativity. Weak links do not pose the same obstacles to new combinations of resources and ideas. Many more options are available. Places with weak links are more open and accessible to newcomers and social outcasts. They are vital to creative processes. According to Florida (and urban researcher Jane Jacobs before him), they are basic components of 'creative capital', an umbrella term for the conditions that reward creativity in a particular place.[17]

Florida's studies of the characteristics that are peculiar to creative centres in the United States have aroused the interest of Nordic researchers. Public officials, administrators and planners, especially at the regional and local level in Sweden, have also been drawn to his work. A recent doctoral thesis examines Swedish, Danish, Finnish and Norwegian studies that have been conducted in the spirit of Florida's writings.[18]

As with the American works described above, the basic hypothesis of Nordic studies is that technology, talent and tolerance generate creative

capital that stimulates dynamic growth in particular places and regions. Proceeding from the same
questions, similar methodologies and comparable
databases are subsequently used. As in the United
States, various urban regions of the Nordic countries are classified on the basis of selected indicators. The few minor differences stem from access
to statistics and the like. For instance, Nordic
studies lack the number of patents as a measure
of technology and the percentage of homosexuals as a measure of tolerance. By the same
token, Nordic researchers classify their indicators according to 'business climate' and 'people
climate'. Interviews sometimes supplement the
statistical analyses.

Macro-analyses of four Nordic countries include
14 urban regions – four capital regions, four
regional centres and six smaller regions. More
detailed studies of Swedish conditions divide
the country into 70 labour market regions. Such
classification systems most closely resemble the
breakdown into metropolitan areas used in the
United States.

The results of these studies show that Florida's
theses of creative centres have but limited appli-
cability to a Nordic setting. Only the four capital
regions meet the American criteria of creative
settings and places. Such discussions are largely
irrelevant to rural and regional centres, or to
smaller regions.

There are several reasons for these differences
between American and Nordic society. Each

Nordic country has only one metropolis with more than one million inhabitants. The United States has 50 such cities. Influenced by the abundant English literature, Nordic social scientists and planners tend to ignore that fact. Moreover, immigrants are far less represented in the creative class of the Nordic countries than of the densely populated regions in the United States.

Generally speaking, the Nordic workforce is less mobile. The employment market for highly skilled specialists is very small. Job openings are generally limited to capitals and university towns. Women are much more likely to work, which means that a couple must find two jobs in the same place. Many people must choose a place that offers a wide variety of jobs, not one that would be the most attractive if lifestyle and other noneconomic factors prevailed.

The Nordic countries are considered to be welfare states. Social and economic gaps are narrower than in many other countries. Ambitious policies, particularly in Sweden, and effective measures to distribute income as uniformly as possible have kept regional differences relatively small. Education, health care, elderly care, childcare and other services are available in all regions, although their quality and accessibility may vary somewhat. In light of the discussion presented in Chapter 4, the question may be asked as to whether uniformity and social equality inhibit creative processes.

5.3 Breeding grounds of renewal

Studies of contemporary metropolises as breeding grounds of creativity and innovation reinforce the observations of Chapter 4. The economic and cultural role of cities has been relatively static over time. At various periods of history, cities have assembled both economic and creative capital. That remains the case today, even if different places are in the limelight. The urban landscape of creativity changes, but the conditions that promote innovative processes endure.

As opposed to homogeneity and uniformity, cultural diversity and variation favour creative processes. Openness and tolerance facilitate progress, whereas narrowness and fanaticism inhibit it. Even when there are seeds of strong links between people, temporary networks must be encouraged. Flexibility and diversity pave the way for new combinations of ideas and experiences. Economists have demonstrated that track-bound development can stand in the way of innovative processes.[19] Among the advantages of big cities is that they offer people multiple tracks to follow. They have stations and switchyards at which different currents of thought intersect, providing multiple opportunities for cross-fertilization.

Human capital is the most important ingredient of creative capital. The places in which creative people choose to live and work offer the basic conditions for renewal. Periods of mobility tend to precede local and regional outbreaks of creativity.

Political conditions have periodically spurred widespread immigration. But the labour market has generally been the determining factor.

Entrepreneurs and creative people have moved to places that offer markets and job opportunities. Recent discussions about the propensity of people to relocate have stressed noneconomic incentives. American research has found that members of the creative class are often guided by lifestyle and other personal interests. Such trends are not as pronounced in the Nordic countries.

This chapter has treated creativity as a very broad concept. Genuinely creative people and original ideas are as rare as gold in a prospector's pan. You have to wash the pan for a long time before finding the grains. This book will now proceed toward a narrower concept of creativity when examining the accomplishments of individuals. Meanwhile, it is important to look closely at the difference between productivity, efficiency and entrepreneurship on the one hand, and genuine creativity and innovative ability on the other.

6. The institutional milieu

Cultural and institutional diversity, markets, customers, physical density, and good transport and communication are among the attributes of successful cities. They offer arenas for human interaction, a basic prerequisite for renewal. Places with such characteristics that are able to attract creative people – whether for economic, lifestyle or other personal reasons – may turn into leading centres of innovation.

This book has so far discussed the qualities that distinguish creative milieux at a very general level. It is worth noticing, but it is certainly not surprising, that characteristics of significance for creative processes can be detected in the diversity and variety of big cities, in their human encounters and myriad of activities. The question arises as to the usefulness of regarding contemporary metropolises as uniform, cohesive settings. A big city is like a jungle that is rich in biological diversity and hosts a wide range of species. The details are only partially visible, narrowing the options for an in-depth understanding of creativity and its prerequisites.

As aforementioned, profound insight into the external preconditions for creativity is mostly available from examining small organizational units and clusters of people who collaborate and compete with each other. They are niches of innovation in an urban environment, scattered like islands of creativity in a sea of more traditional activities. Small groups of creators in art, music, literature, technology and science gained renown at one time or another for their accomplishments in Florence, Vienna, Berlin, Paris and London – and in New York, Boston, San Francisco and other cities, more recently.

In addition to creative collectives, this book reviews what has been written about firms, universities and other organizational units whose settings stimulate or inhibit creativity. Two questions are of particular interest. The first question involves the form and size of an institutional setting. The second question concerns the short-term tension that may arise between an organization's needs for both creativity and productivity.

6.1   Form and size

Before offering a few examples, a discussion in principle will prove useful. Such a discussion centres on different forms of organized collaboration among individuals. Groups of artists, writers and other intellectuals – particularly artist collectives in smaller places and idyllic settings – might be added to the urban environments recognized in previous chapters. All of them share certain common features. They are informal and governed by few rules. They are held together by meeting

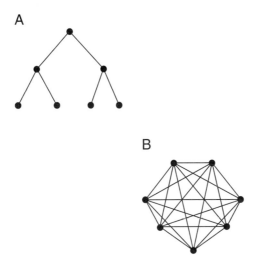

Figure 6.1   *Hierarchical and egalitarian organizational forms*

places and communities of interest. While some close-knit networks last for decades, they usually dissolve after a few years. They are characterized by flexibility. They frequently consist of an inner circle that attracts an ever-changing group of cosmopolitans. Many such groups have been acclaimed as breeding grounds of renewal, both historically and in the contemporary world.

The organizational forms of firms, other organizations, public agencies and institutions of higher education and research are much more regulated, often governed by rules and even legislation.

Figure 6.1 is a useful starting point for an initial discussion about the advantages and disadvantages of different organizational forms, particularly in terms of facilitating creative processes.

The forms shown in the figure represent two extreme poles. Most institutions and workplaces these days are structured according to principles that fall somewhere in-between. The elementary diagram is intended for use at various organizational levels. While entire concerns or universities may be involved, this book will apply the diagram to individual workplaces and departments, as well as small teams of employees and researchers (see Chapter 9).

The two fictional organizations in the figure each include seven nodes (people, workplaces or other units) that are linked (dependencies or contacts) in various ways. Organization A is hierarchical in structure. The transmission of information, orders and tasks follows formal, top-down channels. Bottom-up, but not horizontal, transmission is also possible. Organization B is an egalitarian, sometimes referred to as flat, form. People have direct, unmediated contact with each other. The purest type has no superiors or subordinates.

Human capital is equal in the two organizations shown by the figure, assuming that all nodes possess the same skills. But social capital is much greater in B than A. An assessment of creative capital must consider variations of competence among the people involved in a particular example. Backed up by a lot of the literature, we assume that creative capital has better prospects of growing in an egalitarian than in a hierarchical organization.

The hierarchical form resembles a military organization in which orders and the chain of command – from the commander-in-chief to various officers down to privates – are clear and rapid. For the large-scale armies of the nineteenth and twentieth centuries, that was an efficient way of synchronizing the movements of different units and maintaining morale.

Rank in an army is based on a hierarchical structure of units – corps, divisions, battalions, companies and groups. Businesses may follow similar principles. A chief executive officer, along with a management team, is in charge of middle-level managers. A manufacturer may have foremen who supervise and allocate tasks on the shop floor. Firms have divisions and departments just like the military.

Bureaucracy is sometimes used to denote strict decision-making hierarchies, particularly in the public sector, which strive to ensure continuity and fairness. Universities also have a hierarchical structure that varies little from country to country. A vice-chancellor and administrative director collaborate with the vice-chancellor's office and a central administration. Under them are faculties and sections led by deans and their offices. At the bottom of the ladder are departments and special centres. Senior management in firms normally works with a board of regents, which is ultimately responsible for the owners. In universities electing boards at each level of the organization is a common practice. The universities of some countries are nationally supervised by a ministry and other government agencies.

Two questions are important in this connection. The answers are crucial to identifying the organizational forms that promote and those that inhibit innovation. The first question concerns the extent to which creativity and innovative ability are dependent on the size of an organizational unit. The second question involves a possible conflict between efficiency and productivity on the one hand[1] and innovative ability and creativity on the other. Important to note is that any such conflict is only short term in nature – a politician's term of office or an executive or civil servant's period of appointment. If they want to be re-elected or re-appointed, they have to show quick results. But the benefits of an invention or innovative process may not manifest for a long time. It is not always easy to demonstrate the value of long-term thinking.

A hierarchical organization may become very large. It can grow to a global concern without losing its cohesiveness. An egalitarian organization is more modest. It must remain small in order to retain its distinguishing features. A simple calculation demonstrates the limitations involved. Seven nodes require 21 links. A hundred nodes require 4,950 links, and 1,000 nodes require 499,500 links. Problems associated with the growth of a flat organization may be resolved in two ways – either by transition to a more hierarchical structure in which most information flows are one-way, or by dividing up the organization. A combination of the two approaches is likely to be the most feasible.

A hierarchical organization has its advantages. It is efficient and manageable for the foreseeable future. But it poses clear obstacles to renewal. An egalitarian organization is less productive in the short run but possesses qualities that are integral to a creative process. There is a growing awareness that more flexible organizational forms and associated opportunities for change are difficult to achieve, given that control and stability have been the primary objectives up to this point. The philosophy of secure, predictable, well-planned and efficient activities is deeply rooted and has shaped many of the values associated with industrialism. Administrative tools such as studies of working methods, network planning, operational research and logistics are among the most refined manifestations of this focus on control and security.

A bureaucratic organization is often unable to generate radical renewal because its purpose is to control behaviour in order to render it as reliable and predictable as possible. Such an ideology may view creative behaviour as undependable. Greater creativity in a bureaucratic organization requires less rigid structures, decentralization, more open communication, a project orientation, rotation of tasks, teamwork, regular restructuring and egalitarian rather than authoritarian management.

Experience shows that it is very difficult to deliberately construct a creative milieu. However, such a setting can be easily destroyed by strict regulation and control. In retrospect, a great deal of radical innovation has occurred *against* the will of established institutions and organizations. Gaining a hearing for new ideas in large organizations is a particularly formidable challenge. There are many cases of successful change projects that were carried out after innovators outmanoeuvred or outwitted the formal structures. Pioneers have gone far beyond their authority to acquire information, resources and support. They have built coalitions and networks outside of rigid hierarchies.[2]

A well-established approach to promoting the innovative potential of large organizations is by breaking them down into smaller, independent entities, some of which take charge of routine, 'productive' activities while others assume responsibility for research and development. The first group of entities is often hierarchically structured. The second group is flatter. Small firms and other organizations can ensure renewal by replacing management and restructuring from time to time. The next section in this chapter (Section 6.2) discusses how organizational forms that favour creativity can over time successfully interact with those that are more productive in the short run.

First, here are a couple of examples of how big firms break down their organizations into independent entities that make fundamentally different demands. These examples illustrate the conditions that characterize the geography of a knowledge-based economy. In this economy research and development account for a growing percentage of the value added, associated with manufacturing and trade. The manufacture, wholesaling and retailing of pharmaceuticals and electronics are good cases in point. The ingredients of a new medication or the components of a mobile phone or computer are not of considerable value in purely pecuniary terms. The economic value of the products, as well as the prices they command in the market, reflect underlying research and development, which may have taken many years and involved highly educated specialists and other employees.

The headquarters of a research-intensive enterprise A (see Figure 6.1) are normally located in or around a metropolis. Managing a business from such a location has its advantages. Research, represented by the next level in the hierarchy, is conducted in places that have universities and research institutes, which provide training relevant to the project in question. The lowest level contains the units that manufacture and handle goods. The availability of cheap labour often determines where these units are located.

Approximately 60 per cent of the Nordic pharmaceutical industry is in the Øresund region, forming clusters of big and small companies in addition to research and health-care units. Most of the remaining industry has sprung up in the Stockholm area, including Uppsala and Södertälje. Proximity to the University of Copenhagen, University of Lund, University of Uppsala and the Karolinska Institutet has been integral to that concentration. Businesses have taken advantage

of research conducted at universities and institutes. Even more important has been the ability
to hire highly qualified specialists in the immediate vicinity. A large percentage of employees at
the research units of pharmaceutical companies
have postgraduate degrees. Such proximity has
also made it easier for scientists to move between
the laboratories of universities, research institutes
and firms. Some companies have relocated their
research activities abroad when skilled scientists
were not available in the Nordic area.

Nokia, which began manufacturing mobile
phones in Finland in the early 1980s, is now
the biggest producer worldwide. With its head
office in Esbo on the outskirts of Helsinki, the
company has upwards of 100,000 employees in
120 countries. More than 21,000 are engaged in
research and development. Finding researchers
and qualified electronics engineers has always
been a major problem. Initially, the University of
Helsinki was the only place in Finland that offered
the required training. When research and training started up at a new university in Uleåborg
on the Finnish side of the Bay of Bothnia, Nokia
relocated some of its operations there (currently
some 3,500 employees). At the beginning of the
century, the company conducted research and
development around the world, including in Palo
Alto in the southern Silicon Valley. Nokia collabo-
rates with the Helsinki University of Technology,
the Tampere University of Technology, Stanford,
MIT, Cambridge and the University of Glasgow.[3]

Sony Ericsson Mobile Communications is a major competitor of Nokia. The company produces fewer mobile phones but also has a worldwide organization. Its international headquarters are located in London. The company has far-flung manufacturing and marketing operations. It conducts research and development in Britain, the Netherlands, India, China, the United States and Sweden. Most of its 2,300 employees in the Swedish university town of Lund are engaged in research and development. They are constantly designing and developing new models to be manufactured elsewhere. Propinquity to the university is necessary, though not sufficient, when it comes to finding specialist expertise. Software engineers are recruited from India and other countries. Sony Ericsson now has its own complex in Lund but began at the Idéon Research Park, which is closely associated with the university. A couple of hundred other businesses are presently located at Idéon. Many of them are small and just getting started. They operate in diverse sectors but are all research-intensive. Idéon is an excellent illustration of the way that university research and higher education can spawn new enterprises in their immediate vicinity.

Employment conditions and location patterns of the businesses described above are constantly changing, as is the case for many of their counterparts around the world. Technological progress, demand trends and competition require flexibility and adaptation. Statistical data from various sources are soon obsolete.

6.2   Can creativity and productivity be reconciled?

Any conflict between productivity and efficiency requirements on the one hand[4] and innovative ability and creativity on the other is short term in nature. An analogy will illustrate the point.

Figure 6.2 shows a river that flows through a stylized landscape. The slope of the terrain initially causes the river to flow rapidly in a specific channel. That is a 'stable' phase. Further down, the landscape flattens out. The river flows slowly and enters what physical geographers call a bifurcation zone. It begins to flow outwards and seek alternative channels. Its flow can be easily affected during this 'unstable' phase. If it is dammed up, an oxbow lake forms.

The flow stops. Embankments may be built to

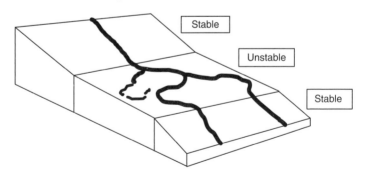

Figure 6.2   Stable and unstable phases of development

ensure continuation of a previously stable and controllable flow. Alternatively, channels can be dug in new directions. Finally, nature may be allowed to decide. Figure 6.2 assumes that no human action is taken. The river finds its way back to sloping terrain. It can dig two new channels on its way to the sea. It is stable once again.

Creative milieux come and go. Firms and scientific institutions, places and regions are rarely hotbeds of transformation for more than relatively brief periods of time. But the same place and institution may come back and attract interest during different periods. Scientific breakthroughs, medical progress, new technology, artistic renewal and fresh styles appear in both temporal and spatial clusters. The older historical examples described earlier in this book often extended across long epochs, up to several hundred years, whereas most of the more recent ones are significantly shorter. Artistic eras lasted for 30 to 40 years from the twelfth to the eighteenth centuries, and for an average of 18 years in the eighteenth and nineteenth centuries. A generation of artists is now regarded as innovative for eight years, and a new one appears every five years.[5]

Focusing on an individual institution, place or region, the structural instability required for radical change appears as a cyclical course. Stable and unstable periods alternate over time. During a stable phase in the world of art, a new direction makes its breakthrough, sets a trend and becomes accepted by broad, influential groups. A stable phase of science is dominated by uniform theoretical approaches. Researchers prove their theorems, experiment with elegant hypotheses and refine their methodologies. But they do not call their basic assumptions into question. Standard research generates a large output as measured by the number of publications. A stable phase of industry is viewed as productive and expansive. Sales go well and share prices rise. Previously developed products are marginally improved. Manufacturing is streamlined. Given growing demand, there is no need for radical innovation.

An unstable phase is initially characterized by stagnation and irresolution. Various ideas and styles begin to clash. Scientists discover more and more exceptions to their basic assumptions. Conventional wisdom and authority are questioned. Disciplines shift paradigms. Industrial sectors experience crises, and disciplines experience stagnation. But in rare moments and at fortunate places, irresolution and searching eventually lead to renewed success and stability. Researchers design fresh paradigms and industries develop new products, technologies and organizational forms. Universities and firms reap the rewards of previous transformation and innovative thinking.

Proceeding from the above line of reasoning, the causes of both stagnation and renewal should be sought in an earlier phase than the one in which they appear. The literature demonstrates that stability and uniformity generally lead to stagnation at one point or another. Successful research and artistic activity congeal into fixed forms. Expansive firms devote all their resources to maximizing productivity but are quick to neglect comprehensive product development. From that point of view, an unstable phase is beneficial from a longer-term perspective, even if very painful for many of those who are directly involved. In our history we can point out broken lives during such phases. Events get out of hand and disaster ensues. But unstable phases have also provided the opportunity that many pioneers were waiting for. Skilled innovators able to take the initiative have great latitude to act in a hesitant, unstable milieu.

The above discussion also implies that efforts to gauge and compare the success and excellence of various organizations and institutions at a particular point in time are highly dubious. It is easy to overestimate and be blinded by the quantifiable results of units in a stable, productive phase, while – due to measurement difficulties and insufficient transparency – ignoring auspicious activities conducted in a setting that is in a risky, creative phase.

7. The scientific revolution

The role of scholars has evolved from ivory tower seclusion to active participation in social development. This chapter is devoted to science and research as engines of contemporary economic growth. While somewhat peripheral to the central theme of the book, the overview serves as an introduction to subsequent chapters, providing a transition from the general discussion of creative environments to analyses of particular research settings, including a detailed examination of the concept of innovation.

7.1 The great breakthrough

Science pervades all modern social evolution. But there is also a trend in the opposite direction. Assessments of research and higher education often proceed from efficiency criteria and models originally designed for firms. The material foundations of economies, societies and cultures are as profoundly affected by current scientific progress as they were by the industrial revolutions and new technologies of the eighteenth and nineteenth centuries. As Manuel Castells writes:

> It follows a close relationship between the social processes of creating and manipulating symbols (the culture of society) and the capacity to produce and distribute

goods and services (the productive forces). For the first time in history, the human mind is a direct productive force, not just a decisive element of the production system.[1]

Research and development account for a growing percentage of the value added, associated with manufacturing and trade. The trend – along with the expansion of formal education and the esteem that science and research enjoy among wide swaths of the population – reflects the growth of a knowledge-based economy. The information generated by research is not only expanding in absolute terms but penetrating segments of society that were not directly affected in previous epochs.

The extension of formal education is one of the most distinctive trends in advanced industrialized economies. Sweden's rise from one of Europe's poorest countries to one of its richest in less than a hundred years was accompanied by an increase in average education from three to eleven years for the working population. University training expanded rapidly after World War Two. Before the 1930s and 1940s, fewer than 1 per cent of Swedes attended what are now referred to as colleges and universities. By the end of the century, the figure had risen to almost 50 per cent. Universities for an exclusive elite have become higher-educational institutions open to all.

Ever since the nineteenth century, higher education and university research have been chiefly financed and regulated at the national level. In countries like Sweden, the leading employers of

university graduates have been the Church, education system, health-care system and public administration. As economist Nathan Rosenberg has
demonstrated, there was little crossover between
science and industry until the late nineteenth
century. Even later on, science and industrial technology went their separate ways despite many
common sources and joined forces only now and
then. Not until well into the twentieth century did
innovation systems emerge that indirectly linked
businesses and institutions of higher learning. The
recruitment of university graduates to research
laboratories of the private sector represented the
first modest crack in the wall.[2]

World War Two brought the great breakthrough. Much of the scientific and technological
capacity of the belligerents was devoted to total
war. The Manhattan Project was the most impressive example of close cooperation between science
and the war industry. Experts with varying
ethnic backgrounds were brought together in
secret laboratories. Research that would have
required decades in peacetime was completed
within a couple of years. Entire industrial towns
for research and development were built in the
wink of an eye. Never before had such enormous
resources been devoted to expanding the frontiers
of knowledge.

A gigantic space research programme subsequently emerged in a similar, though less structured, form. During the Cold War, collaboration
between industry and science intensified in the

US, the UK, France and many other countries. The strongest links are still often within the military-industrial complex. Among similar complexes are the food and health-care industries.

As the above trends proceeded, much of the population became aware of the practical role that sciences played in national growth and development. The aura and prestige surrounding researchers were brighter than ever before. Eventually that reassessment applied to all fields of research, not only physical science and medicine. The notion that universities are important catalysts of technological and industrial progress is widely held these days. Public debate generally proceeds from the assumption that there are fundamental correlations between research, education and the global competitiveness of the private sector – and thereby a country's level of employment and welfare.

Knowledge production and science were traditionally associated with universities and specialized research institutes. Projects were conducted according to hierarchical organizational forms, within fairly isolated disciplines and under strict quality-assurance procedures. The autonomy of universities and the independence of scientific research from the outside world were viewed as valuable and useful. The world that is emerging in the early twenty-first century is not conducive to a strict division between research and other aspects of social life. Science, politics, economy and culture interact in ways that make for extraordinary complexity. Different factors have become so internally heterogeneous and externally interdependent that they are no longer clearly discernible. Scientific knowledge is not limited to certain places and sectors but is rather socially distributed. Viewing science as an isolated phenomenon is not particularly meaningful any more. Analyses, calculations, theories and abstract models are not the exclusive tools for the staff of universities and research institutes.

Many circumstances have conspired to create this social distribution of knowledge and research. Universities are now designed for the masses instead of the chosen few. In some countries, half of young people attend institutions of higher learning. University graduates hold a growing number of positions in a wide range of professions. Experts are not affiliated with universities and research institutes only. More and more of them work in the public and private sector as well. Independent specialists, consultancy firms and groups of experts channel knowledge and skills from traditional academic research to the rest of society. Informal contact between researchers, experts and decision-makers generates complex networks in which ideas and information can be transmitted. The characteristics of contemporary knowledge production may be summarized as follows:

1. The number of places and settings in which new knowledge can emerge is on the rise – not only colleges and universities, but independent

institutes and research centres. A growing percentage of research is conducted at corporate laboratories and development divisions. Both the private and public sector engage experts and consultants with postgraduate degrees.

2. Places and settings are linked by well-functioning electronic, organizational and social communication networks, as well as informal personal contact.

3. Knowledge is increasingly differentiated and specialized. Areas of expertise are constantly reconfigured into new spheres of knowledge, which tend over time to depart from the traditional breakdown into distinct disciplines.[3]

The emergence of a more open system of knowledge production coincides with greater complexity in society as a whole. Both tendencies may be regarded as manifestations of growing uncertainty. Social development is no longer seen as predictable. Post-war confidence in planning peaked several years ago. Three events were seminal in that respect: the oil crisis of 1973–74, the collapse of communism in Eastern Europe and the end of the Cold War, and the terrorist attack on the World Trade Center and Pentagon on 11 September 2001.

7.2 The third mission

The primary missions of universities have traditionally been research and education. Many observers have accorded great importance to the institutional links between the two commitments. In recent years, extensive debate has centred around a third mission – not only furnishing society with a well-educated workforce and disseminating knowledge about significant research findings, but acting as catalysts of economic growth, as well as local and regional development. Research and higher education are expected to serve regional policy initiatives the same way that manufacturing industry once did. Decisions made within the university system – along with local, regional and national public officials – have been influenced by such arguments. The following discussion will touch upon the results of research conducted on the basis of opinions voiced during the debate.

Various successful and dynamic regions and places around the world house important universities and research institutes. The international literature frequently offers large, densely populated regions as examples. A number of studies have been published about regional milieux in the US, Europe and Japan. This discussion will be limited to a few early, well-known cases. The settings share a number of common characteristics. They are densely populated, feature large universities and research institutes, and have a significant hi-tech industry, particularly sectors related to electronics and information technology (IT). The research findings permit identification of two distinct groups of settings.[4]

The first group includes the London–Heathrow–Reading corridor, Plateau de Saclay just south of Paris, Sophia Antipolis near Nice, the Munich region, the Kista–Arlanda corridor north of Stockholm and the Tsukuba Science City near Tokyo. These areas are characterized by a great concentration of hi-tech firms. Leading universities and research institutes are located in or near them. But studies have not found any clear synergies between university research and the business community. Despite their close proximity, the two worlds have little contact. Finally, the research and business activities of the regions have expanded rapidly as the result of extensive planning and regulation.

The second group includes Silicon Valley and Stanford University, the Highway 128 complex around Boston and MIT, Aerospace Alley and the Cal Tech in the US, and Cambridge in the UK, with its venerable university and new research centres. These settings enjoy significant synergies. Knowledge and information are directly transmitted from university research to clusters of firms. A number of university units and research institutes compete with each other. There are bountiful institutional and individual networks, which are held together by key persons who are well acquainted with each other. The settings are loosely regulated, essentially unplanned and the products of a relatively long growth process.

Those who have studied the environments

concerned point to the following circumstances to explain the conspicuous differences among them. Synergies do not become visible for 10 to 15 years, at the earliest. In order for them to emerge, university research must be in sync with the needs of industry, as was the case during the Soviet and US space programmes and the Cold War. The defence industry has frequently played a key role. In the background have been people whose early initiatives sparked a long-lasting chain reaction. The collaboration of scientists and entrepreneurs has been characterized by close, elaborate contact. Such coordination has been based on mutual understanding and trust.

The case studies that have been published show that there are no simple answers to the question of the role that research and higher education play in local and regional environments. The literature offers examples of universities that serve as engines of regional growth and development. But it also presents cases of universities and firms that are not dependent on each other at either the local or regional level. Studies of Swedish conditions provide support for these findings.[5]

The fact that two phenomena – such as successful research and industrial expansion – appear in the same area does not necessarily point to a causal relationship between them. A set of circumstances that appear to be propitious in one place may not have the same impact elsewhere.

7.3 Clusters and innovation systems

The concepts of 'clusters' and 'innovation systems' have recently attracted considerable interest within some branches of economic and geographic research. The concepts are closely related and are used to analyse various transformational economic and industrial processes. The components of the systems of interdependencies studied involve manufacturing, service, administration and research. Both clusters and innovation systems may be regarded as milieux in which institutional units of the kind discussed in previous chapters and those to be presented in the next are embedded, mutually dependent on each other.

Based on the work of Joseph Schumpeter, Chapter 3 made a distinction between the concepts of invention and innovation, both of which are transformational in nature. But one difference is worth noting. Invention refers to a *primary* discovery or creation, something that is fundamentally new and specific. Innovation concerns a *secondary* process and is based on previous discoveries and creations. A creative process consists of the events and actions that precede a primary invention, whereas an innovative process consists of those that follow it. The two processes together represent the chain of events that ultimately generate change. Pioneers embody the first process and entrepreneurs the second one. Entrepreneurs bring the ideas of pioneers to the market. They are proficient innovators but rarely groundbreaking inventors.

At one time, a linear model was frequently used to describe the role of university research prior to and during an innovation process. The chain of cause and effect was simple and straightforward. Basic research was the first link. Research was assumed to occur primarily at universities and technical institutes, largely financed by government grants. Applied research elaborated on the results of basic research, sometimes under the aegis of a university, but increasingly at industrial laboratories and research divisions financed by private sources. The last step involved the development of new products and processes that could be used commercially and create new job opportunities, ultimately improving general welfare. The linear model did not assume any geographic proximity between the various links. Basic research might be conducted in one place, product development in another and application somewhere else entirely, perhaps far away. But models gradually evolved that stressed the importance of physical proximity. MIT, Stanford in the US and Cambridge in the UK became normative in that respect.

The linear model is still relevant in certain connections. But it often presents an overly schematic and simplified view of the complex relationships inherent to contemporary knowledge-based economies. More intricate models are beginning to delve deeper into the impact of research on economies and welfare. Innovative processes are assumed to occur during interactive learning with a number of activities and different parties involved. Innovation systems refer to the structures that replaced the simple cause–effect chain of linear models. Innovation systems are networks that link institutions together, or agents who know and trust each other. Among them are researchers at universities and other institutions, decision-makers in the public sector and employees in various types of firms. Analyses of typical technological innovation processes occasionally employ terms such as technological systems and technological clusters.[6]

Innovation processes are often extraordinarily complex. Many firms, institutions and individuals may be involved in an interplay of dynamic forces. Identifying the most important sources of knowledge is not always an easy task. Researchers stress two types of sources of information. The first source is based on scientific research and is referred to as 'analytic'. New products and manufacturing processes appear on the road from basic to applied research. Scientific research is of particular relevance in this regard. Among such research areas are genetics, biotechnology and IT. The second source of knowledge is based primarily on engineering know-how in manufacturing and is referred to as 'synthetic'. It is generally found in production-building on the application of well-established findings and various combinations of them. Among them are segments of the machine, engineering and ship-building industries.

'Cluster' is a fashionable word these days. The term made its breakthrough in the early 1990s, particularly in the works of American econo-mist Michael Porter. He argued that international economic competition involves firms rather than nations. Porter described the way that competi-tiveness is created within clusters of related firms and supporting activities, including subcontrac-tors, distributors and customers. Among them are also universities, vocational schools, trade organi-zations and public bodies that provide special-ized training, information, research and technical assistance.[7]

Porter's work bears significant similarities to the theories of French economist François Perroux, who coined the term *pôle de croissance* (growth pole) to refer to sectors or groups of businesses in a national economy that are strongly linked to each other. Growth in such a sector has significant ripple effects throughout the economy. A growth pole is actually a point of intersection between sectors (rows and columns) in an input–output table.[8] Neither Perroux nor Porter initially lent the above concepts any specific geographic sig-nificance. They were used simply to indicate that businesses were components of functionally cohe-sive systems, regardless of physical distance.

Use of the term 'cluster' to refer to a particu-lar geographic setting that links businesses and support services together has become common in recent years. The subcontractors, customers, competitors, universities, organizations and public agencies of a region may be included. Among the best-known clusters are Hollywood in the film industry, Silicon Valley in IT, Detroit in the automobile industry and London in finance.[9] In connections where geographic proximity plays an important role, the term 'regional innovation system' is used today.[10]

7.4   Forms of communication

The information and knowledge that circulate in both clusters and innovation systems spur transformation. Information about new discoveries and constructions is disseminated, stored, upgraded and applied to generate economic benefit. Knowledge bases grow in places where experience is assembled. The research mentioned in the previous section distinguishes between tacit and codified information and knowledge.

Tacit knowledge is based on experience gained at a workplace through observation, oral instruction and concrete collaboration. People within sight of each other cultivate dexterity and technical skills. Vocational schools and institutions for practical engineering play a key role in conveying tacit knowledge. Researchers who stress the importance of tacit information generally draw their examples from manufacturing firms. But such information has a significant impact in other fields as well. Take the artistic training offered by drama schools, art academies and music conservatories, as well as medical training in clinical settings and postgraduate work at laboratories and other facilities that have state-of-the-art technical equipment.

Codified knowledge can be written down and thereby, as opposed to the oral tradition, preserved and communicated to many people without changing its content. Instructions and manuals are attempts to teach practical skills in a codified form. Anyone who has tried to follow such directions realizes that this type of knowledge transmission has its limitations. How complicated would a manual on how to ride a bicycle be?

Tacit knowledge – imitating and being instructed by someone who possesses the requisite skills – has clear advantages. Most clusters and innovation systems that have been studied involve a complementary relationship between tacit and codified information, and knowledge.

8. Universities in focus

Chapter 3 discussed various types of scientific personalities. The pioneer or trailblazer and the academic entrepreneur or organizer represented two poles on a continuous scale. Anyone who has long moved in academic circles knows how rare genuinely creative researchers are and how the system tends to favour entrepreneurs. But the system also features a third kind of researcher, who might be referred to as the keeper. They have a broad overview of a discipline and are able to summarize disparate research findings, manage the entire body of knowledge and serve as a valuable source of information, particularly for instructional purposes.

One person may possess the characteristics of all three types of researcher. But ordinarily a number of people collaborate to form an organization that has the intellectual and creative capital required for success. Such capital takes a long time to build up and may quickly dissipate. Most scientific milieux contain a combination of a few pioneers and a greater number of entrepreneurs and keepers.

The discussion of Figure 6.2 in Chapter 6, with respect to stable and unstable phases of development, is highly relevant to an in-depth analysis of various research settings. Breeding grounds of scientific innovation come and go. Although the renown of radical trailblazing processes is passed down through literature and oral tradition, they often last for only a short period and are associated with a few particular people. However, the same place and institution may recur and attract interest during different eras.

8.1   Measuring excellence

How can scientific proficiency and innovative ability be measured in order to identify settings that may be described as excellent? Objectively assessing new research findings when they are first presented is an impossible task. Inherent to the work of pioneers is that it is ahead of its time. Contemporaries may lack the tools required to critically assess a pioneer's hypotheses or findings. For instance, Nobel Prizes are generally awarded to ageing scientists for contributions they made when relatively young (see Chapters 11 and 12).

Assessments of research and higher education generally proceed from quantitative methods. Academia has incorporated various efficiency criteria and models originally designed for firms. In education, the ratio of applications to admissions and the number of graduates are frequent gauges of productivity. When it comes to research, assessment commonly stresses the number of published reports and the frequency with which works are cited in the literature.

Academia has always used evaluations of

research reports and scientific articles as a basis for judging qualifications, often according them decisive importance when making appointments. Quantity – in terms of publications and active participation at conferences and symposiums – has acquired greater importance in recent years with respect to promotions and grant applications. International acclaim is also assigned special importance. The productivity, as measured by such criteria, of research and higher education has increased. That has been a boon for many of the departments and institutions involved. Whether genuine creativity has benefited from the new assessment methods is still an open question. As pointed out in Chapter 6, it may be a conflict between productivity and creativity – seen in a short time perspective.

A number of warnings have appeared. Quantity can for the moment become a more important measure of excellence than quality or innovative ability. A recent report by the Research Strategy Committee of the Royal Swedish Academy of Sciences speaks of the publish-or-perish syndrome. Curricula vitae tend to contain more and more titles, many of which are reports and articles of little originality or interest.[1]

However, a considerable portion of quality assurance is built into the system. Theses must be defended publicly. But if no grades are assigned, as is the case in most of Sweden, differences in quality may go unnoticed. Not until experts examine qualifications during appointment processes are researchers truly compared with each other. Publishers may engage experts to review manuscripts that have been submitted. Scientific journals use a referee or peer-review system of editorial committees and specially appointed experts.

Researchers submit short reports to a large number of scientific journals in various disciplines, the great majority in English. This approach to quickly disseminating research findings was initially limited to medicine and certain scientific disciplines. Now it is increasingly common in many social sciences, and even the humanities. The success of *Thomson Reuters*, an American company, illustrates the scope of such activities. The company compiles and distributes bibliometric statistics – the number of works published, individually or co-authored, and the number of citations in the literature. The data, which covered approximately 8,700 journals in 2008, are available from the *Web of Science.* They can be broken down by researcher, team, university, institution, discipline and geographic area. While the standing of the various journals varies, the most reputable within each discipline are generally included.[2]

Scientists who are frequently cited in the literature are considered to be successful. Whether their renown reflects genuine creativity, diligence or efficiency, organizational ability cannot be determined on the basis of bibliometric data alone. For that, close knowledge about the individual researcher is needed. This is a topic worthy of further study.

Another question that needs to be addressed is how long individuals influence trends in their particular disciplines. The limited data currently available suggest that acclaim tends to come and go during short periods of time, as indicated by the extent to which their work is noted in the literature. Recall the cycles that individual research milieux experience – waves generated by a few scientists who have been associated with them for a limited period.

Historian Eva Österberg, an esteemed teacher and researcher at Lund University and highly experienced when it comes to grant foundations and research committees, has criticized the system harshly:

> Unfortunately, the idiom of the business model has assumed control over thoughts and actions. A surprising number of people, even at universities, have accepted the idea that research can be evaluated by means of statistics on the number of articles cited, as calculated by commercial organisations in the United States that are subsidised by big international journals. Absurdly enough, financially weaker journals in Europe and all books by humanists, social scientists and others are left out – in the first case because they cannot afford to pay for inclusion in the database; in the second case because monographs are either wholly excluded or are not written in English.
>
> Similarly, the idiom of the business model wreaks its havoc when universities fire staff or close departments due to 'unsatisfactory production' of full-time students or annual articles, regardless of whether they possess teaching expertise that the university should have for more profound cultural reasons. The freedom of university researchers and teachers must include a mode of thinking and speaking about what we do that preserves the

fascination with creativity and respect for the long-term search for a deeper understanding of complex connections. It takes time to delve beneath the surface, whether in English or other languages, thick books or short articles. Ultimately the path of knowledge is towards greater and greater depth.[3]

8.2   Ranking

Academia has always harboured subjective views about the relative status of different universities. Some institutions have been perceived as more prestigious than others. Research conducted at certain places has been assigned superior quality. However, systematic attempts to rank colleges and universities according to purportedly objective methods are relatively new. It all started off in the United States of the early 1980s. The phenomenon spread to Europe and ultimately to parts of Asia. Sweden first tried to rank universities in the 1990s. While most lists are national in scope, some global versions are now available as well.[4]

A common form of ranking is based on *quality* of education at various colleges and universities. Lists of results are a kind of consumer information leaflet aimed at applicants for admission or at prospective employers. Newspapers, universities, public agencies and other organizations conduct such studies. Education statistics offer various indicators on which rankings can be calculated: the ratio of applications to admissions, the number of graduates, the percentage of foreign students, the number of teachers per student, formal teaching

Table 8.1   Academic ranking of world universities

Indicator	Weight (%)
Alumni of an institution winning Nobel Prizes or Fields Medals in Mathematics	10
Staff of an institution winning Nobel Prizes or Fields Medals	20
Number of staff members highly ranked in Science Citation Index or Social Science Citation Index (SCI)	20
Number of papers in *Nature* and *Science* during the past five years	20
Number of papers published in the Social Science Citation Index during the past year	20
Academic performance relative to institutional size	10
TOTAL	100

Note: The table covers 500 universities.

Source: Institute of Higher Education, Shanghai Jiao Tong University.

qualifications, etc. Surveys of the attitudes of students and teachers, as well as information about the external environment in different university towns, may provide additional data.

For this book, attempts to rank universities on the basis of *research* are of particular interest. Many national lists have taken such an approach. However, there are relatively few international lists that proceed from extensive surveys. An examination of a couple of them will illustrate the differing criteria that are applied. The well-known lists compiled each year by a Chinese institute (Table 8.1) accord particular importance to the

Table 8.2   Times Higher Education *QS World University Rankings*

Indicator	Weight (%)
Peer review scores by international scientists	40
Review of university by international firms	10
Citations in citation index/ number of staff members	20
Share of foreign teachers	5
Share of foreign students	5
Staff members/students	20
TOTAL	100

Note: The table covers 400 universities.

Nobel Prizes, reflecting their international prestige. The other criteria on which the institute relies are the number of published articles and citations in the literature.

A corresponding British survey (Table 8.2) uses non-bibliometric criteria as well. Evaluations by international scientists are assigned great importance. There are clear parallels with current experiments involving panels of experts to examine departments and institutions at universities in Sweden and other countries. The British survey also tries to assess educational quality. A third survey, which is limited to European universities and is based on bibliometric data only, was designed at Leiden University in the Netherlands (The Leiden Ranking) on behalf of the European Union (EU).

For a complete presentation of the results of

various surveys, refer to lists on the Internet.[5] Below are a few general observations.

Regardless of method of measurement, the various lists agree in certain basic respects. Domination by American universities is striking. Among the 100 top-ranked universities according to the criteria of Table 8.1, 58 were in the US. Only two European universities, both of them British, were among the top 10 (see Table 8.3). However, a number of other British institutions score very well on lists that cover Europe only. The question that arises is the extent to which English research is favoured, given the role of the language as the lingua franca of our era. Besides the English-speaking countries, the list in Table 8.3 contains several prominent universities in Japan and Europe. Among the Nordic universities that perform well in most rankings are the University of Copenhagen and the Karolinska Institutet.

The rankings are not particularly stable. The same institutions generally appear at the top from one year to the next. But further down, where differences are small, rankings constantly change. The criteria also affect the results. For instance, Lund University scores fairly poorly due to the fact that no Nobel laureates were associated with the institution at the time the prize was awarded. Lists that consider bibliometric data only place Lund University right behind the Karolinska Institutet.

It is impossible to objectively measure and compare academic excellence. Objections can be

The geography of creativity

Table 8.3   Academic ranking of world universities, 2010

a. The world's top ten

Rank	University	Country
1	Harvard University	US
2	University of California, Berkeley	US
3	Stanford University	US
4	Massachusetts Institute of Technology (MIT)	US
5	University of Cambridge	UK
6	California Institute of Technology (Cal Tech)	US
7	Princeton University	US
8	Columbia University	US
9	University of Chicago	US
10	University of Oxford	UK

b. Top ten in Europe

Rank	University	Country
1	University of Cambridge	UK
2	University of Oxford	UK
3	University College London	UK
4	Swiss Federal Institute of Technology (ETH)	Switzerland
5	Imperial College London	UK
6	University of Paris 6	France
7	University of Copenhagen	Denmark
8	Karolinska Institutet	Sweden
9	University of Manchester	UK
10	University of Paris 11	France

c. Top ten in Asia-Pacific

Rank	University	Country
1	Tokyo University	Japan
2	Kyoto University	Japan

Table 8.3 (continued)

c. Top ten in Asia-Pacific

Rank	University	Country
3	Australian National University	Australia
4	University of Melbourne	Australia
5	Osaka University	Japan
6	Nagoya University	Japan
7	Tohoku University	Japan
8	Tokyo Institute of Technology	Japan
9	Hokkaido University	Japan
10	National University of Singapore	Singapore

Note: For ranking criteria, see Table 8.1.

raised to any attempt that is made. The challenge is to design better methods of measurement. Exaggerated faith in publication statistics and bibliometric analysis has been widely criticized. Each discipline presents its research findings a little differently. Many observers argue that the methods currently in use favour the sciences, engineering and medicine. The humanities and most social science disciplines come up short. That imbalance becomes particularly obvious when significant weight is assigned to the Nobel Prize.

9. Research milieux *par préférence*

The previous discussion about breeding grounds of creative processes asked whether it is meaningful to treat big cities as cohesive settings. The same question can be raised with respect to universities and large research institutes. An in-depth review reveals that centres of radical renewal and excellence are usually restricted to individual departments or teams of researchers rather than entire institutions. They are creative islands in the plethora of activities and projects that colleges and universities pursue these days. The literature describes a number of such oases.

9.1 Focal points of renewal

Researchers are generally able to identify settings that are pre-eminent in their particular disciplines. But surveys of social scientists and humanities researchers demonstrate that the actual institutions are not the important units, strictly speaking, but a handful of people who are or have been affiliated with them for a certain period of time.[1]

The results differ when it comes to scientific disciplines for which research relies on expensive equipment. Take the European Laboratory for Particle Physics (CERN) outside of Geneva, Institut Laue-Langevin in Grenoble and the Rutherford Appleton Laboratory outside of Oxford. Large accelerators and neutron sources of this type (currently planned or under construction in the US, Japan and Europe) require billions of euros in capital expenditures and are used by thousands of scientists around the world.[2]

Following is an account of some scientific milieux that the memoirs of celebrated researchers in various disciplines have pointed to and that the literature has described (also see Chapter 10).[3] Louis Pasteur founded the Pasteur Institute of Paris in the late nineteenth century. It grew to become the laboratory of brilliant scientists, the source of innumerable discoveries, and a Mecca for scholars in the fields of microbiology, biochemistry and experimental medicine. Pasteur surrounded himself with enthusiastic, energetic researchers. According to François Jacob, the joint winner of the Nobel Prize in Physiology or Medicine 1965:

> The typical Pastorian remained long on the periphery of official structures and of an official career. He was a doctor without a practice, a pharmacist without a dispensary, a chemist without an industry, an academic without a chair.

The institute was largely funded by private donations, along with public and private subsidies. As a foundation, it enjoyed great manoeuvrability and flexibility. A number of prominent researchers in various scientific disciplines have been associated with the institute, which had its heyday after World War Two. Everyone who visited and subsequently wrote about it described a setting characterized by constant communication among researchers with various geographic and scientific backgrounds – a stimulating world of competition and scepticism, as well as mutual tolerance and trust.

The Basel Institute for Immunology was a paradise for biomedical scientists of the 1970s. Academic freedom, abundant resources, the absence of ingrained bureaucracies, and a reputation for stimulating collaboration attracted many prominent people. The Roche pharmaceutical company funded the institute from 1970 to 2000. A conventional organizational structure of divisions, departments and units was initially envisaged. But Niels Jerne, the first director, embarked on an entirely different path. He designed a flat structure of equal members. Jerne's elitist notion of science was apparent in his choice of staff. A *single* brilliant researcher was more important than a host of mediocre ones. But once a researcher had been hired, he had almost total freedom to choose his own topics and methods. Jerne encouraged communication by hiring a large staff and squeezing them together. The concept of continuous dialogue and irreverent sharing of ideas is reminiscent of Niels Bohr's ideal for his institute.

Following World War One, the Institute for

Theoretical Physics was built in Copenhagen with Niels Bohr, a subsequent Nobel laureate in physics, as its central figure. Many pioneers of the new physics – including Werner Heisenberg, Erwin Schrödinger (who coined the expression *'Der Kopenhagener Geist'*, or 'The Copenhagen Spirit'), Paul Dirac, Wolfgang Pauli, Max Born and Albert Einstein – made pilgrimages there in the 1920s and 1930s. Leading chemists and biologists visited the institute as well. Though far from a brilliant lecturer, Bohr was able to discover and support promising researchers. His strongest skill was dialogue with colleagues and students, either one to one or in small groups. The give and take of ideas and opinions nourished the creative process, generating powerful synergies.

The Copenhagen Spirit reigned again at the Cold Spring Harbor Laboratory on Long Island, New York in the US. The pioneers of molecular biology gathered there periodically during the 1940s and 1950s. Max Delbrück, the central figure, wrote:

> The 'bacteriogfag group' wasn't much of a group. I mean it was a group only in the sense that we all communicated with each other. And that the spirit was open. This was copied straight from Copenhagen, and the circle around Bohr, so far as I was concerned. In that the first principle had to be openness. That you tell each other what you are doing and thinking. And that you don't care who has the priority.

The University of Cambridge boasts of many Nobel laureates.[4] Like most other universities, it consists of faculties, departments, centres and laboratories. But much of its academic life is linked to its colleges, where instructors and students interact and share meals. The dining rooms serve as meeting places that rival conference rooms and laboratories. The university is particularly famous for its contributions to mathematics, physics, chemistry, biology and philosophy. Its strength is the ability to attract the most brilliant minds in various disciplines. Once they arrive, they have abundant opportunities for communication and collaboration, not to mention fierce competition. Researchers come and go. Only the leading ones manage to stay and thrive in such a setting.

Historian and sociologist Rogers Hollingsworth at the University of Wisconsin has studied all Nobel laureates in biomedical disciplines since 1901. He also examines other researchers who made groundbreaking discoveries in the same or associated fields. His reports are based on more than 200 in-depth interviews, oral accounts, archived material, studies conducted by others and scientific articles. He devotes particular attention to the Rockefeller Institute for Medical Research and California Institute of Technology, both of which are highly successful research milieux.

As opposed to organizations that were originally tied to great scientists and their particular areas of research, the Rockefeller Institute for Medical Research focused on biomedical diversity from its very beginning in the early twentieth

century. Simon Flexner, the first director, stressed
the importance of the cross-pollination of ideas.
One of the institute's outstanding qualities was
its ability to recruit researchers who had been
shaped by different cultures, systems, schools and
working environments. Flexner developed a management style characterized by a flair for detect-
ing promise in others and the ability to obtain the
financial resources needed to attract such people.
In addition, he possessed strategic foresight and a
knack for creating a setting that promoted critical
examination, encouragement and support.

The success of the Rockefeller Institute has been
ascribed to a culture of intensive communication. Daily interaction in varying constellations
spurred intellectual and social integration:

> Intellectual and social integration were maintained
> at Rockefeller Institute by a variety of devices. Eating
> meals together while conversing about serious scien-
> tific matters was an important part of the Rockefeller
> culture and an important means of integrating the
> scientific diversity and depth of the Institute. There
> was invariably high-quality food at lunch, served at
> tables for eight. The idea was that a single conversa-
> tion could take place at such a table, but not at a larger
> one. The degree of intellectual and scientific diversity
> was much less at the Rockefeller Institute than that at
> the colleges of Oxford and Cambridge, where eating at
> 'high table' was also an important part of the culture.
> At the English colleges, diversity ranged all across the
> board (e.g., from archaeology and as well as ancient and
> modern languages to chemistry, physics, biology, and
> mathematics). Apart from lunch, scientific integration
> was also facilitated by the weekly conference everyone
> was expected to attend, at which Institute investigators

or distinguished scientists from all over the world reported about their work.[5]

Like the Rockefeller Institute, the California Institute of Technology (Cal Tech) was a new type of organization when it was founded in the early twentieth century. Though a university, it had no departments – only units – and remained a relatively small workplace. By 1929, the university was regarded as a leading centre for research in physics and chemistry – later in biology as well. Among the well-known scientists associated with Cal Tech was Linus Pauling, the 1954 Nobel laureate in chemistry. The integrated, interdisciplinary culture that emerged at the university was of decisive importance for his thought and research findings. In a similar way as the dining room at the Rockefeller Institute, Cal Tech's famous Athenaeum dining room facilitated the cross-pollination of ideas. Once again, many of the tables seated a maximum of eight people. The university eventually became a world-leading centre of interdisciplinary biology, particularly genetics, as well as successful physics and chemistry research.

The Sveriges Riksbank Prize in Economic Sciences in Memory of Alfred Nobel was established in 1968 and first awarded in 1969. The prizewinners are chosen by the Royal Swedish Academy of Sciences in the same way as the Nobel laureates in physics and chemistry. What makes the prize particularly relevant to this chapter

is the fact that it has so often been awarded
to researchers affiliated with the Department of
Economics at the University of Chicago. They
have to a great degree contributed to the university's top international ranking (see Table 8.3).
The Chicago School of Economics has become
an established concept. Among the Nobel laureates associated with that school have been
Tjalling Koopmans, Milton Friedman, Theodore
Schultz, George Stigler, James Buchanan, Harry
Markowitz, Merton Miller, Ronald Coase, Gary S.
Becker, Robert Fogel and Robert Lucas. Visitors to
the department have described it as cosmopolitan
and vibrant. A number of biographies speak of
Nobel laureates that worked in the same building,
sometimes in the next room. The setting stimulated the 'opening of new worlds'. The contact
network that emerged from that intercourse has
lent the Chicago School of Economics enormous
influence in economic research.

Conferences play a vital role when it comes to
science and academic research. Most disciplines
hold conferences on a regular basis. They allow
researchers to make new contacts and set the
stage for future collaboration. Among the most
influential are the Solvay Conferences. The first
one was held in 1911, and the twenty-first in 1998.
The first seven are legendary because they coincided with the breakthrough of quantum physics.
Albert Einstein and Niels Bohr attended some of
them, Marie Curie all seven.

9.2   Network milieux

The notion of successful research has traditionally proceeded from individual scientists and
their accomplishments. With their groundbreaking ideas and discoveries, Galileo (1564–1642),
Newton (1642–1727), Darwin (1809–82) and
Einstein (1879–1955) are revolutionary figures in
the history of science. Nevertheless, many of their
most-noted research findings were based on the
thoughts and experiences of others. According to
hearsay within the scientific community, Newton
once remarked that: 'We are dwarfs able to see
further than giants in former times only by standing on their shoulders.' The work of great scientists has mostly been nourished by contact with
contemporary researchers and their ideas, but
normally history remembers only the individual
who published the findings.

Well into the twentieth century, prominent
researchers almost always wrote their own
reports. Co-authorship was a rare phenomenon.
The system of promotions and tenure at universities contributed to the situation. Colleagues, both
living and dead, appeared in bibliographies and
footnotes but generally remained anonymous to
outside observers. Imagine isolated stars in a
schematic sky (A in Figure 9.1).

Ever since the 1960s, research findings have
been based on collaboration among members
of a team. Particularly in scientific, medical and
certain social science disciplines, co-authorship

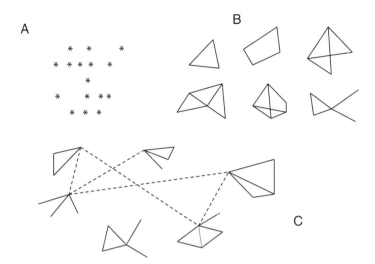

Figure 9.1   Solitary stars and scientific networks

is on the rise and has frequently become the norm. Networks of various sizes are more and more visible. Teams of researchers publish joint reports, their names in alphabetical order or based on seniority, renown or contributions to the project.

B in Figure 9.1 shows a schematic network whose nodes are at the intersection of the various links. Suitably constituted nodal networks permit researchers with differing resources, ideas and skills to complement each other. Creativity is stimulated by contact and cross-pollination among specialists who collaborate on problems of common interest (synergies). Academic entrepreneurs may play an important role in this connection. Primary networks ordinarily remain quite small. They achieve a critical mass for the current objective, setting the stage for efficient division of responsibility among as many specialists as possible. But they cannot get so large that coordination costs become prohibitive. In this context it is important to observe that rigid networks ultimately may create an incestuous interaction of stale ideas and approaches.

The prospects for scientific breakthroughs improve when primary networks are linked together, when individual teams of researchers are embedded in larger collectives. A few key people – often, experienced researchers and prominent entrepreneurs – may take advantage of contacts outside the primary network (the dashed links in Figure 9.1, C). They serve as hubs in a primary network while coordinating contact with others. Thus, isolated schools of thought become part of a more extensive research setting.

Two articles in *Science* examine the network settings described above and the mechanisms that govern them. The studies were based on network theory and quantitative analysis of extensive statistical material. The models they used contain three parameters of particular interest to the present discussion: network size, the percentage of established researchers with far-reaching contacts (veterans) and the percentage of less experienced researchers (rookies).[6]

Table 9.1 presents the empirical material, broken down by discipline. Each discipline is accompanied by figures showing the volume of production and the number of people who

Table 9.1   *Production and participants in networks over time*

Subject/ discipline	Period	Number of productions and publications	Number of participants
Broadway Musical Industry (BMI)	1877–1990	2258	4113
Social psychology	1955–2004	16 526	23 029
Economics	1955–2004	14 870	23 236
Ecology	1955–2004	26 888	38 609
Astronomy	1955–2004	30 552	30 192

actively collaborated in different constellations for 50 years or longer. BMI stands for the Broadway Musical Industry, the number of musicals staged from 1877 to 1990. Excluding actors, upwards of 4,000 composers, librettists, choreographers, conductors, directors and producers worked in close collaboration on more than 2,000 productions during that period. The average number of people in charge of a production rose from two in 1877 to seven in 1979, and remained constant for the next 25 years.

Table 9.1 covers four areas of research. Each discipline is accompanied by the number of peer-reviewed articles published and the number of co-authors involved. The material includes a large number of articles and researchers. The same researchers may be co-authors of more than one paper. The data were taken from 32 scientific journals – seven in social psychology, nine in economics, ten in ecology and six in astronomy.[7] Each discipline can be followed from the 1950s until the early 2000s. The results are strikingly unanimous when it comes to the composition of primary networks. For each discipline, the average number of co-authors rose from one to four.

The *Science* articles go one step further and examine the researchers who participate in various networks. Many networks are composed of rookies along with a few veterans. They can build on experience of previous research projects and take advantage of old contacts who are now members of other primary networks. The authors refer to this dynamic in terms of 'invisible colleges'. Teams of researchers (primary networks) that are particularly successful contain a number of veterans who collaborate with rookies. Teams of well-known people with far-flung contacts are likely to publish more frequently in top-ranked journals, while other teams must be content with less prestigious periodicals.

Successful scientific research, as well as artistic production, is increasingly the result of teamwork and close collaboration. The primary networks responsible for such projects are relatively small (typically four to six people). These small networks work best if strategically linked to larger collectives. Such networks often cross institutional lines but are less likely to be interdisciplinary in nature.

9.3 Characteristics of importance

The settings described in the memoirs of successful researchers and other literature share certain common denominators. Characteristics regarded as conducive to creative processes recur time and again in these writings.

Skill

Like various types of artistic activity, successful research exhibits certain elitist tendencies. Highly skilled researchers are a fundamental precondition for a creative process. Settings that provide a rallying point and platform for such researchers improve the prospects of development and innovation. Generally speaking, researchers with solid skills in their particular discipline are best positioned to ask the right questions. They know where to draw the line between various disciplines and can judiciously step over them into the unknown. Prominent researchers who launch collaborative efforts do not need to have similar skills. On the contrary, those who complement each other on the basis of differing backgrounds find themselves in an advantageous position. Diversity and variation favour innovation processes, whereas excessive uniformity inhibits them. But assembling cutting-edge expertise in one place is not always sufficient to get a process off the ground.

Communication

Accounts of successful research efforts constantly stress the importance of contact and information sharing. More than ever before, the world of science is a powerful communication system. Research and the accumulation of knowledge are based on the dissemination of ideas and circulation of information. A creative process recombines pieces of information, often in surprising ways. Instruction transmits new findings to others. Scientific networks and communities have monitoring, criticism and recognition functions in addition to conveying ideas and perspectives.

Books continue to represent the quintessential method of scientific communication. That has increasingly been the case since the invention of the printing press in the mid fifteenth century (see Chapter 2). Books can be stored, disseminated, read and re-read by many people. They facilitate evaluation, reflection, monitoring and critical examination. Much of the recognition that researchers gain is based on what they write. More scientific books and articles are written today than ever before. Such codified knowledge is supplemented by tacit knowledge transmitted through direct personal contact (see Chapter 7).

Formal collaboration among universities and researchers has increased rapidly. Every college and university worth its salt has international secretariats these days. Whereas most of them had only a handful of collaboration and student exchange agreements with foreign institutions just a few years ago, the figure has frequently risen to several hundred. The EU administers a growing number of agreements and an ever-greater percentage of international research grants. The situation may be described as a jungle of formal relationships whose overall significance is difficult to assess.

In addition to communication arranged by a university, informal contact among individual researchers and ad hoc collaborative projects among remote research settings is expanding even faster. This cooperation is evident from the literature, can be followed through correspond-ence and is supported by lively phone and e-mail contact. In the wake of such information sharing, researchers increasingly get together at working sessions, symposia and conferences. Researchers are the frequent flyers of the academic world.

Researchers have been among the most dili-gent letter writers throughout history. Up until 1970, it was easy to trace the contact networks of individual researchers by examining their cor-respondence. Phone, fax and e-mail contact have gradually replaced letter writing. Each new mode of communication plays a supporting role. Direct personal contact, correspondence and phone calls are all interrelated. Travel is often preceded and succeeded by letters, phone calls, faxes or e-mails.[8]

Conversation and personal encounters are likely to remain the most important means of trans-mitting scientific information, particularly at the beginning of an innovation process. Uncertainty, unpredictability and surprise are inherent to the initial stages of creative processes. At one time, knowledge was passed down from one generation to the next by word of mouth. Socrates wrote nothing that we know of. Plato did, but his teachings reached his disciples at the Academy primarily through his dialogues. For many centuries, his writings preserved the knowledge and wisdom that he had communicated during his lifetime.

The significance of oral communication these days is more related to the etymology of the word 'converse' (Lat. con-verso, to be together). Technical equipment cannot convey all the impressions that direct personal contact permits. All media filter information. Conversation enables immediate response and dialogue. Debate and discussion test arguments and ideas on the spot. The defence of a doctoral thesis is a case in point. Surveys show that researchers devote more than half their working hours to conversation. The number of international conferences, symposia, working sessions and seminars – as well as the number of participants – has increased exponentially in recent years.[9]

Generally speaking, the role of research is still discussed as if it were a national concern only. But research and development are increasingly conducted within international networks beyond the control of individual governments, even though they frequently provide major subsidies. Science has liberated itself from national constraints and operates within network structures that are strongly reminiscent of the Middle Ages. A web of cross-border relationships links different places in an archipelago of universities and researchers. Some places and institutional units become strategic meeting places and centres with a core of key people around whom communication is particularly intensive. Integration and the cross-pollination of ideas through proximity and constant communication are the most common characteristics of the research settings presented in this chapter. But plenty of strategic meeting places have been non-institutional in nature.

In the following, short biographies of some Nobel laureates will be presented. From these the following stories are taken. In them you can find the story of train trips that Niels Bohr took to Germany in the 1920s and 1930s. Colleagues and graduate students lined up at stations that he would be passing through. Hanging out of the window, he would start talking even before the train stopped and would continue to do so after it had started up again while they ran along the platform to catch his parting words. Meanwhile, physicists, chemists and biologists visited Copenhagen to talk with Bohr and see the setting in which he worked.

Werner Heisenberg, a Nobel laureate in physics, recounts that Erwin Schrödinger's health was in danger at one point. Schrödinger and Bohr began talking at the Copenhagen station and continued at Bohr's institute and home. After 24 hours of uninterrupted discourse, Schrödinger collapsed from exhaustion and was bedridden with a high fever. Bohr's wife Margarethe nursed the patient back to health while the two men did their best to carry on the conversation.

Once when Albert Einstein was in Copenhagen, Bohr met him at the station. On the tram to Bohr's institute, they fell into such an intense conversation that they forgot to get off. Realizing their mistake, they headed back in the opposite direction but missed their stop once again. The process was repeated several times before they finally found their bearings.

Scale

Most observers agree that creative processes are born and thrive in small research settings. Information sharing is vital at the beginning of an innovation process, when there is great unpredictability and people do not know each other very well. A wide circle of researchers is hardly conducive to the intensive conversation needed at that point (see the discussion of Figure 6.1 in Chapter 6).

Rogers Hollingsworth argues that the same institutions make groundbreaking discoveries over and over again. Such institutions are generally small but part of larger settings with strong economic resources. Their modest size facilitates close, intensive collaboration. Hollingsworth maintains that many universities are too big to permit significant interdisciplinary communication. They are poor breeding grounds for creative processes. Hierarchical workplaces may be productive and conduct exciting projects without scoring significant scientific breakthroughs. Creativity is best nourished by small egalitarian organizations.[10]

Once a research setting becomes big enough, breaking it down into new institutions and adopting hierarchical and bureaucratic controls is a natural temptation. According to Hollingsworth, such an approach reduces integration and the prospects for major discoveries. But the setting may still appear to be highly productive in terms of publication in scientific journals.

Opinions about the ideal size of a research setting vary. The settings discussed earlier in this chapter typically have teams of four to six researchers. When larger teams of 10 to 15 researchers are required, the importance of achieving a critical mass comes to the fore.[11] Where do you draw the line? Normally at about six researchers – more when it comes to laboratory research and less (three to four) for theoretical research. Some studies conclude that the humanities do not require any such limits.[12]

Innovation processes emerge from complementary settings, each of a different size. Small settings and networks work best if strategically linked to other settings and more extensive networks. Preliminary research reports, conferences and symposia play a major role in that process.

Generosity, equality and competition

A good institution is a stimulating venue for the interaction of ideas and scientific insights. New ideas and impulses may see the light of day at seminars, but informal meetings and consultations at an institution can be even more fruitful. As the Royal Swedish Academy of Sciences points out in one of its reports, generous, loyal collaboration of that type serves as a key complement to the competition that always prevails among researchers and that is an important incentive for scientific progress.[13]

Settings in which transformation and innovation take place often contain an ostensibly contradictory combination of collaboration and rivalry between researchers who belong to an egalitarian elite. One possible explanation is that a sense of social affinity may develop. As equals who are fully aware of each others' abilities, people in such a situation can cultivate trust and tolerance while engaging in competition. But not everyone can accept and play that game successfully. There are stories of research settings that have been regarded as brutal. The challenge of developing a sense of social togetherness while permitting competition without strangling research places heavy demands on institutional infrastructure.

Nils-Eric Sahlin, a Swedish philosopher, writes of his ability to sense the creative atmosphere the first time he enters a new setting:

If you are alert, you can smell the aroma of creativity as soon as you walk in the door. I have had the pleasure of being in a couple of genuinely creative settings. In both cases, I was struck by the hearty laughter – overflowing with productive ideas, fellowship, understanding and human warmth – that bounced off the walls of the corridors and that both surprised and delighted visitors.

I have also had the dubious pleasure of experiencing settings that convey . . . a feeling of suffocation. They smell stale and musty. You feel like opening the windows. And before you know it you're confronted with conflicts that lead nowhere, unfounded accusations, territorial thinking and academic inbreeding.[14]

Researchers in settings where conversation has fallen silent and meeting rooms are empty can easily become loners or seek intellectual stimulation in the type of external network shown in C of Figure 9.1.

Leadership

Creating a supportive infrastructure exacts a great deal from the administration and management of an institution. Management must be fully acquainted with the conditions under which research is conducted. They should also possess solid administrative and social skills. The research settings discussed in this book are often blessed with leaders who are able to create a healthy social atmosphere without extinguishing the desire to compete.

Hollingsworth refers to Simon Flexner of the Rockefeller Institute when describing the qualities of those who have the capacity to successfully lead an institution:

- Strategic vision in order to integrate different areas and conduct goal-oriented research.
- The ability to offer constructive criticism in a supportive and stimulating setting.
- The ability to recruit researchers who are multifaceted enough that the teams in which they participate will be constantly aware of new problems that are amenable to solution and will be flexible enough to take them on.
- The authority and reputation needed to obtain funding.[15]

The physical environment

The settings discussed above are not particularly affected by their physical characteristics: rooms, premises, equipment, etc. Laboratory research, which is conducted in premises and facilities that contain technologically sophisticated and expensive equipment, is an important exception. The accounts of many settings having not devoted much attention to the physical environment may be due to an unrepresentative selection. Another possible explanation is that the creative people who have written about these matters do not assign much significance to their physical surroundings. Regardless of how pleasant or unpleasant they experience their workplace to be, they might not care very much one way or the other. Genuinely creative processes may release inexorable forces that evolve independently of their physical environment.

Descriptions of research settings often speak of overcrowding and meagre offices. Such observations may be interpreted in different ways, depending on the individual's preferences and working methods. Some researchers are able to cultivate their creativity thanks to the lack of orderly surroundings. Others have been able to create despite a chaotic physical environment. Recall the earlier discussion about chaotic conditions in urban environments (Chapter 4).

There is a consistent exception to the above comments about the physical environment: the role played by meeting places, venues for successful personal contact and information sharing. Researchers who have studied the issue maintain that architecture should promote social life. A building should be designed such that there is enough space, not to mention suitable locations, for people to gather. Entranceways, cafeterias and libraries may serve that purpose. Some people have gone so far as to argue that meeting places promote communication more effectively than lecture halls or laboratories.[16] Enthusiastic researchers have always taken advantage of every opportunity for discussion and the exchange of ideas that the physical environment has to offer.

Playfulness and discipline

Torsten Hägerstrand, a geographer at Lund University, sums up the difficulties associated with creating a successful research setting:

> It is not an easy task to design settings that create the latitude for activities that are largely playful in nature but that are kept in check by a particular type of intellectual discipline, especially when large sums of money are involved. Discipline is fairly compatible with an imposed organisation and a certain degree of standardisation. But imagination withers if forced into grooves unless they are spontaneously self-organising. The necessary combination of playfulness and discipline poses a unique dilemma for academic research. There must be room for both ingenuity and nitpicking.[17]

10.   Nobel laureates

The chapter on 'place' (Chapter 4) discussed the ways that pioneers and entrepreneurs have gained renown in various parts of Europe throughout history. Artists, architects, composers, writers, scientists and other intellectuals often achieve fame in places other than their native surroundings. Many of them have been cosmopolitans. Periods of radical innovation have frequently been accompanied by geographic mobility. The same can be said about the people affiliated with the research settings described in Chapter 9.

The next two chapters (10 and 11) focus on the sojourns of researchers and their association with specific places, as well as the dependence of creative ability on various milieux. A number of autobiographies provide the empirical material for this discussion, which is followed by a general analysis of information that can be gleaned from the material.

10.1   Nobel Prize Centennial

Alfred Nobel's will, dated 27 November 1895 in Paris (a year before his death in San Remo), stated the following:

The whole of my remaining realizable estate shall be dealt with in the following way: the capital, invested in safe securities by my executors, shall constitute a fund, the interest on which shall be annually distributed in the form of prizes to those who, during the preceding year, shall have conferred the greatest benefit on mankind. The said interest shall be divided into five equal parts, which shall be apportioned as follows: one part to the person who shall have made the most important discovery or invention within the field of physics; one part to the person who shall have made the most important chemical discovery or improvement; one part to the person who shall have made the most important discovery within the domain of physiology or medicine; one part to the person who shall have produced in the field of literature the most outstanding work in an ideal direction; and one part to the person who shall have done the most or the best work for fraternity between nations, for the abolition or reduction of standing armies and for the holding and promotion of peace congresses. The prizes for physics and chemistry shall be awarded by the Swedish Academy of Sciences; that for physiology or medical works by the Karolinska Institute in Stockholm; that for literature by the Academy in Stockholm, and that for champions of peace by a committee of five persons to be elected by the Norwegian Storting. It is my express wish that in awarding the prizes no consideration be given to the nationality of the candidates, but that the most worthy shall receive the prize, whether he be Scandinavian or not.[1]

Prudent investments have increased the value of the sizeable fund he bequeathed. Its annual yield now finances five prizes worth approximately 1 million euros each. The Nobel Prize celebrated its first centennial in 2001. While awaiting a permanent museum, the Nobel Foundation, which manages the will and fund, arranged a centennial exhibition at the old Stock Exchange in Stockholm.

A copy of the exhibition was shown in a number of different cities around the world from 2001 to 2007.

A total of 806 individuals and 23 organizations were awarded prizes from 1901 to 2009. Two or more people have shared many of the prizes. That tendency has become more pronounced in recent years, highlighting the difficulty of pinpointing the source of a scientific breakthrough. Forty-one of the prizes have been awarded to women, including two in physics, four in chemistry, ten in medicine or physiology, and one in economics.

The following discussion will be limited to approximately 600 Nobel laureates. Winners of the Peace Prize and Prize in Literature have been excluded. Those prizes are awarded on the basis of separate criteria that do not apply to the scientists and researchers who dominate the other categories and constitute the primary focus of this book.

The Prize in Economic Sciences in Memory of Alfred Nobel was established in 1968. Its 63 winners through to 2009 have been chosen by the Royal Swedish Academy of Sciences, the same way as have those in physics and chemistry.

10.2   Why Nobel laureates?

In pursuit of a more profound understanding of the forces that promote creativity and innovation, this chapter examines individual scientists. The examples have been carefully considered. The decision to examine the lives of Nobel laureates was not made lightly. One objection to such an approach might be that the prizes reward achievement in a limited number of disciplines only. Another objection is that equally deserving researchers have been passed over. A tempting alternative was to focus on other disciplines, as well as pioneers in the arts. The final decision was based on the following considerations.

Examining the conditions that promote artistic creativity requires special expertise in painting, architecture, literature, music, philosophy and other disciplines. The author of this book, on the other hand, has long been affiliated with universities, research councils and scientific societies. The focus hitherto on institutional settings for science and research has foreshadowed the orientation of the present chapter. Nevertheless, we have noticed that prerequisites and obstacles to creativity are in many respects similar regardless of the group of pioneers that is the immediate object of study.

Many Nobel laureates in scientific disciplines have been highly creative people. Some of them have been skilled entrepreneurs or proficient, hardworking and goal-oriented researchers. Success commonly stems from a combination of different traits. The Nobel Prizes are awarded on the basis of a selection process that is much more comprehensive and meticulous than university ranking. Furthermore, Nobel laureates represent relatively homogeneous groups of creative individuals who are amenable to comparison.

Nobel Prizes in scientific disciplines are awarded by the Royal Swedish Academy of Sciences and Karolinska Institutet, whose members are leading scientists in their fields. The Academy is broken down into various classes. Class II proposes awards in physics, Class IV in chemistry and Class IX in economics. The work of each class is performed by specially appointed committees, which call in experts when needed. The Nobel Committee at Karolinska Institutet takes a similar approach.

Each year the four Nobel committees issue individual invitations to thousands of scientific academy members abroad and previous laureates, as well as other eminent professors and researchers at universities and research institutes. The lists are frequently revised. The recipients are asked to nominate new prizewinners in their particular disciplines and to briefly explain their reasons for nomination. The committees compile lists of how many times each researcher has been nominated and the discipline represented. An initial screening process is conducted. Experts review the scientific production of a small number of candidates. As opposed to the publish-or-perish syndrome mentioned earlier, the final assessments are generally made on the basis of a few groundbreaking works. The assessments are presented in detailed, comprehensive written reports, which the members of the committees and various classes read prior to the final vote at a plenary session of the Academy. The entire selection process takes more than a year.[2]

A big advantage of focusing on Nobel laureates is that so much source material is available, including biographies in nearly every case. Initially, they were written before the award ceremony, often in collaboration with the prizewinner. Autobiographies became the norm after World War Two. Many have been published as books, and edited online versions can be obtained from the Nobel Museum.[3] Almost 700 biographies, including those of literature and peace laureates, meet the usefulness criteria that have been established. The following discussion will use bits and pieces of that material for illustrative purposes.[4]

Particularly in a study aimed at identifying general rather than individual characteristics, extracting useful information from autobiographies is no easy task. They do not follow a particular template but proceed from the events and circumstances that the authors regard as seminal in their lives. However, most autobiographies contain certain basic information:

- childhood circumstances
- schooling
- higher education
- career
- workplaces
- sources of inspiration
- personal encounters.

Supplementary material is also valuable. Since 1965, Hungarian chemist and physicist István

Hargittai has interviewed more than 100 prominent researchers, 76 of whom are Nobel laureates. The interviews have been compiled in a volume entitled *The Road to Stockholm*.[5]

10.3 Creativity on the move

The international scientific hegemony of the United States becomes clear when looking at the list of Nobel laureates. Svante Lindqvist, former director of the Nobel Museum in Stockholm, has compiled statistics on Nobel laureates of the twentieth century. Figures 10.1 and 10.2 summarize the results.[6]

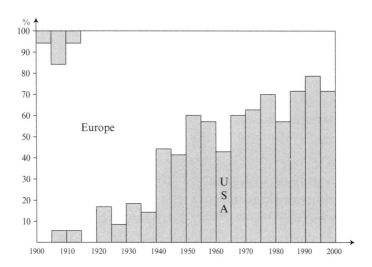

Figure 10.1   Nobel laureates in physics, chemistry and medicine, 1901–2000, broken down by geographic area based on citizenship when the prize was awarded

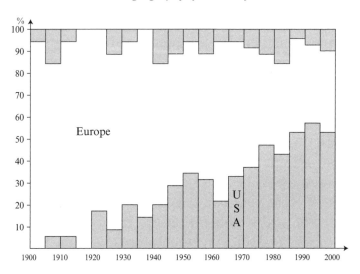

Figure 10.2   Nobel laureates in physics, chemistry and medicine, 1901–2000, broken down by geographic area based on birthplace

European citizens were predominant through the 1900–40 period. The trend shifted towards American citizens during and after World War Two. By the end of the century, their share had risen to around 70 per cent. Laureates from countries outside Europe and North America were relatively rare (Figure 10.1). The breakdown changes somewhat if based on birthplace, as in Figure 10.2, which reflects the same population. European dominance of the prize still wanes, though less dramatically. Not until the end of the century were 50 per cent of Nobel laureates born in the United States. Other parts of the world are represented, though modestly, in nearly every five-year period.

Table 10.1   *Nobel laureates through 2008, broken down by university (with at least 5 each)*

University	Number
Harvard University	24
Cal Tech	17
MIT, Cambridge	16
Stanford University	16
University of Cambridge	16
University of Chicago	15
University of California	15
Columbia University	15
Princeton University	10
Rockefeller University	10
University of Oxford	8
Cornell University	8
Berlin University	7
MRC Laboratory of Molecular Biology	7
Sorbonne University	7
University of London	6
University College London	6
Göttingen University	5
Pasteur Institute	5
Karolinska Institutet	5
P.N. Lebedev Physical Institute	5
Uppsala University	5

Given that Nobel Prizes enjoy such great international prestige, the desire of universities to have as many laureates as possible is hardly surprising. Such figures are heavily weighted in certain rankings. Universities and research institutes frequently refer to the number of laureates who are or have been affiliated with them when recruiting students, soliciting donations and applying for government subsidies. Table 10.1

shows the current breakdown of Nobel laureates by the university with which they were *affiliated* at the time the prize was announced. Laureates in Economics are included along with those in Physics, Chemistry and Medicine. [7]

American universities boast a big lead. Cambridge is the only European university among the top ten. A total of 23 laureates have been affiliated with the university or its MRC Laboratory of Molecular Biology. All other European universities appear in the second half of the list. The results tally with observations in connection with the earlier discussion about attempts to rank leading universities around the world. There are a number of reasons for American hegemony. Given historical experience and the autobiographies that will be presented shortly, one reason is of particular relevance.

American laureates began their ascension after World War Two. Prior to that, German and other European universities and research institutes had the most laureates. More than half of all laureates who have written about their childhoods grew up in rural areas (small or medium-sized towns), and the rest in cities with populations of 250,000 or more. A number were raised in New York, Chicago, Boston and other big American cities, but the great majority came from Western and Central European metropolises such as Paris, Berlin, London, Vienna, Budapest, Munich, Hamburg and Prague.[8]

The term 'brain drain' is relatively new, but the

phenomenon has been around for a long time. Various kinds of artists, artisans, scientists and intellectuals have left their native surroundings throughout history to seek new challenges or livelihoods in thriving international centres.

The quest of gifted persons for education and skills improvement has always been a major incentive when it comes to migration. The journeyman system was an early example. The mobility of artisans was a major contributing factor in creating a cosmopolitan European population before the first Industrial Revolution. During Sweden's period as a great power, nobles sent their sons on 'grand tours'. Pioneers and entrepreneurs of Swedish industry often received their basic education abroad. Artistic trends and innovation have always relied on geographic mobility. Researchers are on the move more than ever before. The next chapter will take up these dynamics in greater detail.

There have been other incentives as well. Capital has often been the decisive factor. Pioneers and entrepreneurs have gone where consumers, markets and economic resources were concentrated. Opportunities for personal and career development are particularly attractive for young people, whereas the availability of economic resources is more decisive for their older, well-known colleagues. This kind of brain drain grew to unprecedented levels during the turbulent twentieth century. However, violence, oppression and political developments were the primary motives rather than career opportunities or financial reward.

Approximately 360,000 members of the Russian intelligentsia and bourgeoisie moved to Berlin in the wake of the Bolshevik Revolution. Among them were many leading artists, writers and scientists. Some 200,000 Russians of similar backgrounds immigrated to Paris, many after having lived in Berlin until the early 1930s. Much of the cultural vitality of the two cities during the interwar years was due to these population movements.

Either voluntarily or under coercion, approximately 400,000 people left Germany or the areas it occupied during the 1930s and early 1940s. The expatriates included thousands of leading scientists, film producers, actors, writers and artists, many of them Jews. Much of Central Europe was depleted of intellectuals. The largest percentage of them went to the United States, contributing to its technological, scientific and cultural upsurge after the war.

11. Scientific careers in time and space

Particularly in our time, the emergence of creativity cannot be predicted on the basis of a specific place. A creative process can be tied to *one* place or *one* institution for a limited period of time only. Nor can it be taken for granted that creative people are affected by the settings where they gain prominence or are temporarily affiliated. Conventional maps are inadequate instruments when the focus of study shifts from conditions to processes.

The observations that appear in various autobiographies have been schematized in several time-geography diagrams. Such diagrams are well suited to identifying common features rather than peculiarities in the lives of different people. Particular attention will be paid to information that recurs in many autobiographies – a record of events and removals that many Nobel laureates regard as having been integral to the development of their creative ability.

11.1 Time-geography

Torsten Hägerstrand of the Department of Social and Economic Geography at Lund University says that he began to think in terms of time-geography back in the 1940s.[1] But the approach did not make its breakthrough until the 1960s. Hägerstrand and a group of doctoral students developed new theoretical tools and expanded the scope of time-geography to include different applications. Gradually, the new approach engaged more and more researchers in Sweden and abroad. A research setting and school of ideas emerged that resembled those discussed in previous chapters with regard to other countries.[2]

As its name indicates, time-geography describes processes in both time and space, simultaneously, with the help of trajectories. A common variant is to follow how individuals move between points of locations, or 'stations'. In these stations no movement occurs in space, only in time. Such analyses are commonly based on 24-hour cycles. Figure 11.1 shows a person's daily trajectory between home and school or the workplace. Up to this point, time-geography is used to describe actual behaviour. Even more revealing is its ability to apply physical realism to analysis of the options offered by a geographic setting that is subject to various human and environmental constraints. However, such applications are beyond the purview of this book.

Depending on the processes and course of events to be studied, cycles other than 24 hours may be used. The following discussion is based on relatively long periods. Time in Figure 11.2 represents all or part of a lifetime. Space has only

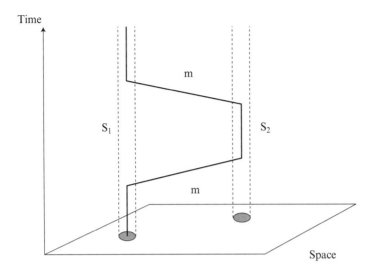

Figure 11.1   Basic concepts of time-geography

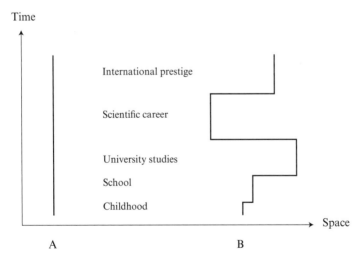

Figure 11.2   Life paths for a stationary (A) and mobile (B) person

one dimension, as opposed to a traditional two-dimensional map. The diagram shows two different life paths, unbroken in time and space from birth to death.

A remains in the same place throughout life. Take the philosopher Immanuel Kant, who reportedly never left Königsberg (now Kaliningrad). B moves several times, living in one place during early childhood, attending school in a second, pursuing university studies in a third, conducting research in a fourth, and achieving international prestige in a fifth.

The most important issue for the purposes of this discussion is to determine which of the five settings cultivate and shape B's creativity. Or is it the combined influence of several settings? If so, does mobility stimulate creativity? This book has described several periods of unusual geographic mobility during which the arts and sciences underwent radical transformation.

Moving from one place to another takes time. In other words, a life path contains no strictly horizontal lines. That is obvious during a 24-hour cycle (Figure 11.1). But travel time is negligible from the point of view of an entire life. Moreover, subsequent diagrams will use what is known as a time filter. Most researchers and Nobel laureates take many trips that may last anywhere from a few days to a couple of weeks. Charting all such movements in this type of time–space diagram would be both impractical and meaningless. Various analyses have required the individual to remain in a particular place for one month, one year or longer.

11.2   Life paths in the twentieth century

As the autobiographies of Nobel laureates make eminently clear, a handful of selected life paths can reflect many of the dramatic events that marked the twentieth century.

Time-geography diagrams should not be over-loaded. Comparing several hundred Nobel laureates in one figure would make it impossible to discern general patterns. Furthermore, lumping together researchers in so many different disciplines is of questionable value. Grouping scientists into certain disciplines for the sake of analysis has been deemed appropriate. The Nobel Museum once exhibited an illustrative model of different life paths. At the bottom of an aquarium-shaped showcase was a map of the world. Golden threads coiled up from points on the map to the top of the showcase. Each thread represented a Nobel laureate in a particular discipline. The exhibit was removed after a while. Visitors had trouble relating to the intricacies of time-geography.

Following are a few examples taken from a large body of material. The graphic presentation proceeds from certain simplified assumptions. The goal is to highlight fundamental lines of argument without getting stuck in the detail.

Figure 11.3 covers the entire twentieth century and essentially the whole world. Along its space

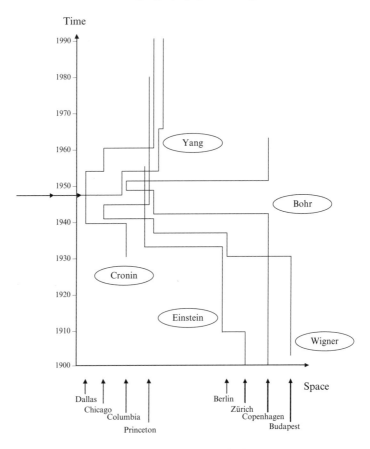

Figure 11.3   Life paths of five Nobel laureates in physics

axis are various places that are relevant to this chapter. For technical reasons, the diagram does not reflect actual geographic distances, though they may be of interest in other connections.

Figure 11.3 shows significant stretches on the life paths of five well-known Nobel laureates. All of them ended up at Princeton University or the

Institute for Advanced Study in the same town. Certain differences between their trajectories are worth noting. Two of them are typical of the most recent Nobel laureates. James W. Cronin was born in the United States in 1931 and worked in Dallas and Chicago before his ultimate affiliation with Princeton. Chen Ning Yang, who was born in China in 1922, does not appear in the diagram until the late 1940s at Columbia University, followed by Princeton and finally at Stony Brook University on Long Island in 1965.

The other three life paths are characteristic of a previous era. Beginning in Europe, they typify a majority of all Nobel laureates. Before Hitler was appointed Chancellor in 1933, only seven Americans had won Nobel Prizes in scientific disciplines. All the others came from Europe. Eugene Wigner was born in Budapest in 1902 and attended one of the upper secondary schools (gymnasia) that will be discussed later in this chapter. After leaving Hungary, he pursued further studies in Germany and obtained a position in Berlin. He immigrated to the United States in the early 1930s and won the Nobel Prize in Physics in 1963 while affiliated with Princeton.

Albert Einstein was born in 1879 in Ulm, Germany. From 1902 to 1909, he worked as an assistant examiner at the Zurich patent office, where he developed his special theory of relativity. He presented the general theory in 1916. His theory of the photoelectric effect, for which he was awarded the 1921 Nobel Prize in Physics, was also published while he was at the patent office. After a time as a professor at the University of Zurich, Einstein directed the Kaiser Wilhelm Institute for Physics in Berlin for 20 years and made many trips to Göttingen. Due to growing anti-Semitism in Germany, he renounced his German citizenship and immigrated to the United States in 1933, where he was affiliated with the Institute for Advanced Study in Princeton. He was regarded as too eccentric for the university. He departed his life path in 1955.

Niels Bohr was born in 1885 and spent most of his life in Copenhagen. He was affiliated with the Institute for Theoretical Physics until leaving Denmark in 1943, as the country had been occupied since 1940. He ended up at Princeton. After the war, he returned to Copenhagen, where he died in 1962. He was the 1922 Nobel laureate in physics.

11.3   Stations on a life path

In addition to academic institutions and research settings, the autobiographies of Nobel laureates and other eminent scientists stress the importance of the homes in which they were raised and the schools they attended. The common features of the autobiographies of Nobel laureates can be summarized in a simple time-geography diagram. Figure 11.4 compiles a dozen life paths. The diagram shows seven stations in time and space where the paths form clusters (highlighted by shaded ovals).

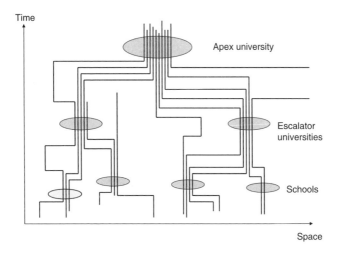

Figure 11.4   *Settings (stations) where life paths form clusters*

These are places with which several Nobel laureates have been affiliated simultaneously. The clusters at the bottom of the diagram represent schools at various levels. Those in the middle represent a couple of universities. We may call them 'Escalator' universities where several scientists have stayed for a time during their careers. The one at the top represents a prestigious university or research institute ('Apex' university) – attractive by virtue of its terms of employment or financial resources – in another part of the world. The diagram offers an overview of the settings that have influenced and shaped many prominent researchers. No cross-section – whether at the top, middle or bottom – of such a diagram can tell the whole story. That would require consideration of the

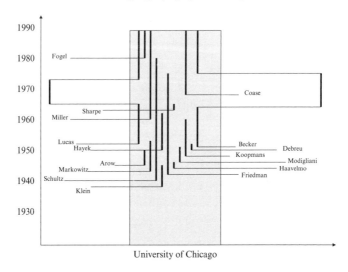

University of Chicago

Figure 11.5   Department of Economics at the University of Chicago – a station for Nobel laureates in economics

ways that a researcher is influenced at various places and periods.

Focus on one setting

Walking up one of the big staircases at the University of Chicago, a visitor encounters an impressive collection of portraits of Nobel laureates. Twenty-two of them received or shared the Prize in Economic Sciences in Memory of Alfred Nobel to 2008. All of them have been researchers or students at the Department of Economics, Law School or Graduate School of Business. Figure 11.5 shows the 16 Nobel laureates who were affiliated with the Department of Economics from the

1930s through to 1990. The department is high-lighted as a station in the middle of the diagram. Everyone in the diagram originally came from another setting, and most of them were born in Europe. After ten years with the close-knit Chicago school, Robert Lucas and Gary S. Becker moved on and after some years came back again. Many more examples of notable settings similar to this department – stations that assemble creative researchers and entrepreneurs – might be presented. A number of them were described in Section 9.1.

Home

The professions pursued by the parents of many Nobel laureates suggest a great deal of intellectual stimulation at home. Approximately one quarter of the laureates had at least one parent who was a prominent researcher, eight of them Nobel laureates themselves. Many were doctors, engineers, teachers or clergy. There are ample studies to show that children of intellectuals are much more likely to pursue higher education than their classmates. Universities have still not managed to correct that imbalance in the recruitment process.[3] More remarkably, and much more difficult to explain, is the fact that a disproportionate share of Nobel laureates (approximately 20 per cent) have been Jews. That is 30 times as many as a random selection would have produced. Thirty-six Jews have won the Nobel Prize in Physics, 22 in Chemistry and 39 in Medicine.[4]

There are probably several reasons for the large number of Jewish laureates. Many European Jewish homes traditionally stressed the importance of studies and higher education. Autobiographies have pointed to a strong sense of family and demanding, supportive parents. The Jewish mothers are often held up as momentous. Feelings of alienation, vulnerability and persecution by the outside world contributed to the cohesion of the family.

After emigration, some Jewish laureates have emphasized the advantages of feeling comfortable in more than one culture. Many twentieth-century pioneers were first- or second-generation immigrants and belonged to a cultural minority. A common observation is that long-time Jewish residents of the United States rarely win a Nobel Prize, and that there was no Israeli laureate in a scientific discipline until 2004. Georg Klein, a well-known Jewish cancer researcher at Karolinska Institutet in Stockholm (originally from Hungary), is frequently asked about that when he is in Israel. His stock answer is: *'Atem b'bayit'* ('You are at home').

School

Autobiographies of Nobel laureates frequently mention the strategic importance of primary and secondary schools in providing the foundation of knowledge and skills that enable creativity later in life. Teachers can awaken the latent abilities of children and influence the direction that their studies eventually take. Poor teachers may have the opposite effect, squashing a student's incipient interest. Even if a child has a basic aptitude in a particular area, outside forces may determine the choice of a specific discipline. A sports analogy illustrates the point. A child might have an exceptional ball sense and great potential when it comes to football, tennis and golf, ultimately choosing one of them due to external circumstances.

Like their counterparts around the world, Central European gymnasia have been fertile breeding grounds for an intellectual elite. This book does not discuss approaches to designing education systems that provide as many students as possible with opportunities for development. But regardless of how particular schools and systems are structured, the competence and inspirational abilities of teachers play a major role in settings where creative processes arise.

The following passages from the autobiographies of Nobel laureates describe the role of teachers, primary schools and secondary schools in their early development. They express their gratitude to the teachers who, familiar with current research, aroused their interest and affected the direction of their future studies. They portray schools so strict and demanding that even the most capable students were challenged. In addition to Hungary, Germany, France and Britain offer excellent examples of such dynamics.

More than 20 of the most celebrated scientists of the twentieth century were born in Hungary and went to gymnasia in Budapest. Most of them attended universities in other parts of Europe and reached the apex of their careers in the United States. Among them are four Nobel laureates in physics, one in chemistry and one in medicine. Others are celebrated researchers in disciplines for which no Nobel Prizes are awarded – for instance, mathematicians John von Neumann, Gabriel Szegö and Paul Erdös. In addition to the scientists are a number of leading writers, performers and artists. Arthur Koestler is one of them, as is businessman and philanthropist George Soros. The various autobiographies of Hungarian laureates identify several gymnasia as models of excellence. Among the most frequently mentioned are the Minta ('model') Gymnasium, the Lutheran Gymnasium and the Piaristorden Gymnasium.

Eugene Wigner (see Figure 11.3) began his 1963 Nobel acceptance speech as follows:

> I wish to say at this occasion a few words on a subject about which we think little when we are young but which we appreciate increasingly when we reflect on our intellectual development. I mean our indebtedness to our teachers. [. . .] We have not only teachers who are older than we, we learn also from contemporaries and younger colleagues. The contemporary from whom I learned most – in fact immensely much – was von Neumann but that was mostly mathematics.[5]

The following passage is taken from Wigner's autobiography:

In 1915 Budapest was filled with fine high schools. But on the wide street called Fasor was located my Lutheran Gymnasium. It was likely the best high school in Hungary; it may have been the finest in the world.[6]

Physicist and mathematician Edward Teller was born in Hungary in 1908. The stations on his life path – Minta Gymnasium, a German university and some of the American universities mentioned earlier – were shared by several others of his generation. He wrote:

Whether it was the educational system or a particular combination of circumstances during those painful years in Hungary, the flowerings of talents from the gymnasia in Budapest is a fascinating field of speculation. An uncanny procession of brilliant men emerged from those troubled classrooms. Most of them were Jewish and many of them made their way to the United States where they contributed mightily to American scientific advancement and especially to the development of nuclear physics and the release of nuclear energy.[7]

The following passage is taken from the biography of John von Neumann, one of the great twentieth-century mathematicians:

John von Neumann went through the early twentieth-century Hungarian education system that was the most brilliant the world has seen until its close imitator in post-1945 Japan. The booming Budapest of 1903, into which Johnny was born, was about to produce one of the most glittering generations of scientists, writers, artists, musicians, and useful expatriate millionaires to come from one small country since the city-states of the Italian renaissance. [. . .]

> The usage of the name 'gymnasium' was borrowed by most of German-speaking Europe, and by any countries that looked to Germany for educational leadership. France called her version a 'lycée', and Britain called its version 'grammar school'. The modern Japanese – who adapted an extreme, and extremely successful, version of the gymnasium system – call their school 'high schools', as if they were just like open-to-all American high schools, which they are not.[8]

Though by no means unique, the above quotations are typical of many autobiographies. Beyond the role of schools and teachers, another common observation is relevant to a discussion of the factors that promote or obstruct innovation in a particular setting. Nobel laureates sometimes mention the tempestuous transformations and challenges that they faced when their surroundings were uncertain and precarious. The summary of Chapter 4 touched upon this observation when discussing concepts such as chaos and structural instability. The following passage from the autobiography of George Békésy (1961 Nobel Laureate in medicine and physiology) is a testament to the importance of such concepts:

> If a person travelling outside Hungary is recognized as Hungarian due to his accent – something which, beyond a certain age, is impossible to drop – the question is asked almost in every case: 'How is it possible that a country so small as Hungary has given to the world so many internationally acknowledged scientists?' Some Hungarians tried to give an answer. For my part: I cannot find an answer, but I would mention one thing. When I lived in Switzerland, all was peaceful, quiet and secure; we had no problems about earning a living. In Hungary, life was

different, and we all were involved in an ongoing struggle for almost everything which we wanted, although this
struggle never caused anybody's perdition. Sometime we
won it, sometime we lost; but we always survived. It did
not bring an end to things, not in my case anyway. People
need such challenges, and these have existed throughout
the history of Hungary.[9]

12. Epilogue

This book has relied on both broad overviews and detailed narratives. It has moved between the macrocosm of major dramatic events and the microcosm of their smallest components. Descriptions of geographic settings and historical developments have presented the larger perspective. The details have emerged when initially defining concepts, discussing social interactions and examining individual biographies. Pitting various theoretical approaches and points of view against each other adds to our understanding of the multifaceted wellsprings of creativity and the complex correlations that tend to characterize significant innovative processes. Fundamental to the book has been the notion of the cross-pollination of differing viewpoints.

Similarly, this summary chapter is structured on the basis of two complementary approaches – all-inclusive and piecemeal. A series of initial questions refocus on the earlier chapters in order of their appearance, followed by a potpourri of details, observations and conclusions taken from various parts of the book. Only when all the ingredients have been arranged in that way is it possible to clearly delineate the book's underlying thematic and logical structures.

12.1 What is creativity and who is creative?

The words 'creativity' and 'creative' are largely artefacts of the post-war era. Having rarely appeared in the German and Romance languages before that time, their use has increased exponentially. Together they generated some 400 million Google hits in late 2008, whereas the words 'innovation' and 'innovative' showed up almost 200 million times. Such widespread use makes it difficult to apply the terms without explicitly defining them. In the colloquial sense, they include everyday resourcefulness, the ability to solve trivial problems, rare genius and everything in-between.

Research on creativity and innovative processes has also taken off in earnest. Different approaches have been pursued depending on the specialties and disciplines involved. Some researchers have concentrated on newly launched products, whereas others have zeroed in on creative persons and the mental process. The geographic and institutional settings, the places, in which creative processes find expression, have been a focal point of this book.

Answers to the question of who is creative can be aligned on a continual scale, one end of which claims that everyone possesses such characteristics and the other end of which argues that they are clustered around a small elite of genuine innovators. Psychological experiments and tests reveal that children are creative before starting school. Then imagination and playfulness subsequently give way to logical thinking and memorization of facts, rules and regulations. The idea that advanced economies are hotbeds for the rise of a creative class has aroused a great deal of interest in recent years. The underlying assumption is that virtually all artists and highly educated people are creative. Many researchers, particularly psychologists and philosophers, have been quick to protest and to advocate a narrower definition of the concept.

Whether involving everyday problem-solving abilities or groundbreaking discoveries, creativity involves similar mental processes. Old patterns of association and thought break down. Creative people have the capacity to shake off ingrained beliefs, tenets and precepts. Researchers of the 1950s began to speak of convergent and divergent thinking. People who think convergently attempt to solve problems in a traditional manner, step by step according to a logical sequence. People who think divergently choose new and untravelled paths.

This book has proceeded as much as possible from a narrow view of creativity. That has lent it an elitist flavour when it comes to deciding who is creative in the profound meaning of the word. By the same token, it has required the identification of people who participate in successful innovative processes though they are not creative themselves. Pioneers, the original creators, are followed by entrepreneurs, who are skilled at recognizing, combining and marketing new discoveries. Entrepreneurs are proficient innovators but rarely groundbreaking inventors.

This book has singled out three different kinds of academic researchers. The real pioneers are few in number and often neglected by their contemporaries – the price they pay for being ahead of their times. Meanwhile, academic entrepreneurs are highly visible, able to assemble, claim and publish new ideas, accumulate financial resources and attract bright students. Finally, keepers have a comprehensive overview of a discipline, along with the ability to summarize and disseminate the findings of other researchers. Only rarely does a single individual possess the qualities that typify all three kinds of researchers. But a scientific milieu cannot succeed unless all these skills are present.

12.2   Where does creativity appear?

Europe, the continent on which this book focuses, has housed geographic areas and places known for remarkable renewal in philosophy, mathematics, art, music, literature, theatre, architecture, technology and other disciplines. This book has used Athens and other Mediterranean city-states of antiquity for illustrative purposes. Florence represented the urban culture that bloomed and the cultural revival that took place just before and during the Renaissance. Industrialism and the revolutionary period from 1850 to 1950 transformed metropolises into major breeding grounds for various innovative processes. This book has identified Vienna, Berlin, Paris, London, Manchester, Göttingen, New York and Boston as the most celebrated of these centres.

Pioneers and entrepreneurs from widely divergent disciplines have achieved renown, often in close collaboration with each other, in such places during different periods of history. Of particular interest to this book is the observation that many of them were born and raised, or worked during much of their careers, somewhere else entirely. Creativity has always been a peripatetic phenomenon, even more so in the modern world. What was the allure that brought creative people to these cities? And what creative potential can be discerned in these and similar milieux?

Economic factors have been decisive. Artists and other creative people find their audiences and their markets where capital accumulates. War and persecution were the leading cause of migration during the first half of the twentieth century. Hundreds of thousands of people fled Bolshevism to settle in Berlin and Paris, while even more escaped from Nazi Germany to various places in the United States. Among them were many prominent filmmakers, writers, artists, scientists and other creative people.

Cultural diversity and venues that promote the informal exchange of ideas have spurred creativity. Meanwhile, a certain degree of institutional chaos has lent pioneers and entrepreneurs greater manoeuvrability. A common observation is that variety and heterogeneity, as opposed to uniformity and homogeneity, benefit creative processes.

12.3   Why big cities?

Ever since times of antiquity, the fortunes of Western cities have reflected economic and cultural development. The same trends and correlations no doubt hold true in other parts of the world. The role played by the cities of antiquity, the Renaissance and the industrial period has been accentuated in the modern world by the emergence of metropolises. Size, the degree of geographic concentration and the scope of various spheres of interest are the main variables that have changed. Moreover, research about these phenomena increasingly focuses on the United States. The post-war tendency to emphasize non-European cities would no doubt be even more pronounced if Japan, China, India and other countries were included. Assuming that the European Union turns out to be successful, the trend may shift once again.

Many of the advantages offered by metropolises stem from their growing importance as centres of finance, power, transportation and communication. Administration and management of firms, financial institutions, research projects, trade organizations and the public sector cluster in the big cities. Institutional density generates a large, diverse supply of services and employment opportunities. Incomes, markets and the number of consumers are greater than in other areas. In both absolute terms, and in relation to number of inhabitants, cultural offerings are even more concentrated in the cities than most other activities. A broad-based, tightly interwoven cultural infrastructure takes shape in the metropolises.

It has been said that creative individuals play the same role in the modern industry as coal and iron once did in the steel manufacturing. US surveys in particular suggest that labour no longer moves to places where employment is available in the manner posited by older theories. The most skilled professionals, including pioneers and entrepreneurs, largely settle down in places where they can pursue their own interests and lifestyles. Firms must start up or relocate to areas in which the most qualified people are living.

Geographic mobility often goes hand in hand with creativity. Places characterized by openness and tolerance promote the accumulation of creative capital. The correlation, described in contemporary studies, between patterns of migration and the dynamics of big cities exhibits clear parallels in European and US history. Immigrants have streamed into the metropolises, where foreignness and a sense of community have intermingled. Important centres have sprouted up in places where differing cultures, religions, lifestyles and political views encounter each other. The metropolises have served as melting pots and focal points for change.

Up to this point, the book was limited to a

general characterization of creative settings. The objection was then raised that a modern metropolis is hardly a homogeneous environment. The innovative forces among such a conglomeration of people and activities are presumably limited to particular niches. To gain a deeper understanding of the conditions that govern and affect creative processes, the book narrowed its line of vision to specific workplaces, institutions, social groups and individuals.

12.4   Can creativity and productivity be reconciled?

The urban environments described by this book offer illustrative examples of the way that small groups of collaborating and competing individuals constitute islands of renewal in a sea of traditionally organized activities. Particularly memorable constellations appeared in Florence, Vienna, Berlin, Paris, London, New York, Boston and San Francisco. All of these groups shared certain characteristics. They were informal and governed by few, if any, rules. Their cohesion derived from common interests and the kinds of meeting places at their disposal in the urban landscape. Closely linked social networks could last for decades but usually dissipated after a few years. Cosmopolitans came and went. Such groups, such as artist collectives, have also cropped up in small towns and pastoral environments.

The book then turned to the obstacles to, and

resources for, creativity that can materialize in firms and public administrations, as well as educational and research institutions. Collaborative arrangements – more regulated, sometimes governed by rules, by laws and legislation – were identified at such organizations. The objectives of many of these organizations are not to prioritize and pursue creativity on a continual basis. Businesses may be hostage to the profit motive. The primary objectives of public agencies are oversight, stability and justice. Secure, predictable, well-planned and efficient activities represent a deeply rooted need that has shaped many of the values associated with industrialism.

The growing insight that flexible organizations facilitate necessary innovative processes posed a dilemma that required the book to look more closely at two particular issues. The first issue concerned the extent to which creativity and innovative ability correlate with the structure and size of an organizational unit. The second issue involved the potential difficulty of reconciling efficiency and productivity requirements with the need for creativity and innovation. Important to stress is that this kind of tension comes into play only in the short term – perhaps during a particular appointment or term of office – not in a longer perspective.

The hierarchical model turned out to benefit uniformity and homogeneity. Activities evolved in that way could be controlled and governed on the basis of one-way instructions and signals. Meanwhile, the egalitarian model promoted multifaceted internal information sharing and set the stage for fertile creative processes. A hierarchical organisation could become very large and ensure heavy output per unit of time or invested resource. In order to work as an egalitarian system, a flat organisation had to remain small while falling short of ambitious targets when it came to efficiency and quick results.

Big firms in particular may face the dilemma of attempting to reconcile creativity with productivity. Among the solutions that have been tried are to differentiate, either spatially or temporally. Spatial differentiation involves the establishment of various independent or semi-independent units. A few large units are in charge of the day-to-day routine, the productive effort. Smaller units conduct research and development near or in the locations to which they are best suited.

Differentiation may also be temporal. In other words, productive and creative phases may alternate within the same organization. Creative settings come and go. Particularly nowadays, businesses and research institutions, places and regions are rarely hotbeds of innovation for more than relatively brief periods of time. This book has thoroughly discussed the cycles that organizations may go through. Waves of development may seem to appear, phases of widely acknowledged success followed by the semblance of paralysing stagnation. The literature clearly demonstrates that stability and uniformity often,

if not always, lead to decay at one point or
another. Successful artistic activity and research
easily congeal into fixed forms. Expansive firms
devote all their resources to maximizing productivity but quickly forget about comprehensive
product development. From that point of view,
phases of uncertainty and low productivity may
turn out to be godsends in the long run. Original
minds have a chance to prove themselves at
such times. Pioneers and innovators may enjoy
greater manoeuvrability in a milieu that is hesitant and unsteady than in one dominated by
hierarchy and uniformity.

12.5   What is so different about successful
scientific milieux?

This book has accorded particular prominence to
research settings. There have been a number of
reasons for that approach. The chief objectives of
such milieux are renewal and knowledge acquisition, the central themes of the book. For many
years, the author has participated in and observed
events and changes in various university departments and other research organizations. His
growing interest was whetted by the literature
that has been published in recent years. However,
the overwhelming reason for the focus is the fundamental role that science and innovation have
assumed as perceived catalysts for contemporary
social and economic development.

Finding methods that objectively measure

scientific skills is a difficult challenge. Identifying genuine originality is even more daunting. New research findings cannot ordinarily be evaluated when they are released. It takes a long time to critically review and assess them. For instance, Nobel Prizes are generally awarded to ageing scientists for contributions they made while relatively young.

Notwithstanding all the obstacles and objections, attempts to compare the quality of different research environments have multiplied in recent years. The evaluations often serve as the basis for allocating resources and ranking universities. Quantitative methods have come to inform such assessments. Academia has adopted efficiency criteria originally developed for firms. Research, the main topic of this discussion, is largely judged by the number of reports that have been published and how often they are referred to in the scientific literature. Ranking of universities sometimes considers how many Nobel laureates have been, or are currently, associated with them. Evaluations and ranking lists of universities around the world all exhibit a similar pattern. More than half of the top 100 are in the United States. The universities of Cambridge and Oxford are always among the top ten. Japanese, Swiss, German, French and Scandinavian universities are further down. Except for the leading institutions, the differences are quite small and the rankings vary from year to year and list to list.

The validity of such methods for assessing

research settings has been called into question. Exaggerated faith in publication statistics and bibliometric analysis has been subject to heavy criticism. The approach to reporting research findings varies widely from one discipline to another. The established methods work to the advantage of scientific, technological and medical research, which is commonly published in short reports that appear in peer-reviewed English-language journals. Meanwhile, the humanities and social sciences get the short end of the stick. The challenge is to devise convenient methods that represent an improvement. This book has been most critical of entire universities and large scientific institutions as objects of study. Generally speaking, only individual departments and research teams within the larger institutions meet standards of excellence and spawn scientific innovation. They are creative islands in the plethora of activities and projects that many colleges and universities pursue these days.

This book has described a number of institutional research settings in Europe and the United States that have served as a focal point for scientific renewal. The accounts have relied on the biographies of Nobel laureates, as well as the data available from research reports and reviews of the literature. Studies based on hundreds of in-depth interviews and conversations with laureates and other prominent scientists were particularly valuable. Today's 'invisible universities', composed of networking researchers with varying institutional associations, backgrounds and qualifications were also analysed. The depiction of such networks proceeded from studies of thousands of collaborative projects and research teams over a period of 50 years in social psychology, economics, ecology, astronomy and other disciplines.

People who have participated in and observed different research milieux tend to portray them in a similar manner. As a result, certain clear, consistent conclusions can be drawn about the characteristics of settings that promote creative processes. All of them exhibit undeniable elitist tendencies. When skilled, imaginative researchers work at the same place, the prospects for creativity and development are good. Those with profound knowledge of their particular disciplines are often able to pose the right questions. They know where to draw the line between various specialties and can sometimes judiciously step over them into unknown territory.

Successful research settings are typified by fluent communication and lively information sharing, both internal and external. A creative process forces ideas and perspectives to confront, test and evaluate each other. Even in a hi-tech society, conversation and personal contact play a strategic role. One key reason is that such a process, particularly at the beginning, is replete with uncertainty, unpredictability and surprise. That makes venues conducive to dialogue even more important. Such venues may be located at the institution or elsewhere. Successful researchers are frequent travellers.

Creativity is best nourished by small egalitarian organizations. Hierarchical workplaces may be productive and engage in extensive, celebrated projects without scoring significant scientific breakthroughs. Nevertheless, small settings thrive when surrounded and supported by big organizations with abundant financial resources. The ideal size of a creative setting varies, but a team of five to seven researchers is common. They work best when strategically linked to a larger community and network. The effectiveness of social communication governs and sets the limits for the size of well-functioning research groups.

Somewhat surprisingly, descriptions of research settings do not generally accord much significance to the actual physical environment. Disciplines that require a great deal of technical equipment constitute the one exception to that rule. Insofar as the overall setting is seen as benefiting creativity, meeting places and common areas – dining rooms, cafeterias and libraries just as often as seminar rooms – tend to be singled out. A reasonable interpretation is that the most important role of the physical environment is to facilitate social contact.

A good institution is a stimulating venue for the interaction of ideas and scientific insights. If you look more closely at such settings, an ostensibly contradictory combination of collaboration and rivalry frequently emerges. In special moments and at fortunate places, generosity, collegiality and competition are able to join forces. The book cited researchers who could smell the 'aroma of creativity', an institution's dynamic atmosphere, as soon as they walked in the door. On the other hand, some departments they visited exuded confinement and spiritual stagnation. Researchers no longer interacted and common areas were deserted.

To function effectively, a research setting requires potent leadership. Heads of departments and institutions need to possess more than just administrative and scientific skills. They should also be familiar with the reservoirs of creativity and successful research. Extensive social skills must come to bear if a favourable working atmosphere is to be preserved while maintaining the proper balance between collaboration and competition. Creating a setting for research that must be playful and disciplined, imaginative and goal-oriented, for true innovation to emerge may be an overwhelming challenge at times.

12.6 What can we learn from the biographies of Nobel laureates?

Associating people with the places where their creativity became known and subsequently written about is a natural tendency. This book has raised objections to that kind of facile approach. Only in exceptional cases can creative processes be linked to a single place or institution. By the same token, it cannot be taken for granted that the conditions under which somebody was working at the time they achieved renown were fundamental to the growth and development of their creative abilities. Such objections may appear to be trivial when it comes to disciplines in which biographies traditionally serve as important source material.

This book's analysis of long-term innovative processes, as well as the experiences and influences of different settings throughout the lifetime of an individual, is based on the biographies of hundreds of Nobel laureates. These particular people were chosen because so much has been written about them, because their creative abilities have been subject to unusually thorough assessment, and because research milieux and scientific creativity are fundamental themes of this book.

The biographies cited span various eras of the twentieth century. To avoid drowning in verbose narratives, the lives of Nobel laureates were classified by means of theoretical methodological tools developed at the Geography Department, University of Lund, under the name of time-geography. As its name indicates, time-geography depicts processes in both time and space, simultaneously. The life paths of Nobel laureates were systematized as unbroken lines in time (the vertical axis) and space (the horizontal axis). Groups of laureates were plotted together for the purpose of identifying typical travelling patterns and meeting places (see Figures 11.1–11.5).

Creative ability, originality and imagination are manifestations of innate and acquired qualities associated with specific individuals. The biographies of Nobel laureates make it abundantly clear how childhood stimuli and influences affected the direction that their lives eventually took. A majority of them had parents with some kind of academic background. The disproportionate number of Jews reflects the role of inner cohesion, as well as external challenges and demands. Persecution and a sense of alienation and vulnerability give birth to incentives as well as erecting obstacles.

Education systems have been of strategic importance. They lay the foundation for the acquisition of knowledge and skills, an important prerequisite for subsequent scientific contributions and innovative abilities. Prominent, respected teachers awoke the interests of future Nobel laureates and influenced what field they subsequently entered. European gymnasia and their equivalents elsewhere served as fertile breeding grounds for the cultivation of intellectual elites during the first half of the twentieth century. This book has followed some of the leading scientists from that era, all of whom had received their basic education at the same gymnasia in Budapest.

That a small number of lives can reflect such dramatic social changes is rather remarkable. Moving abroad to obtain postgraduate degrees and start academic careers was common among those who experienced turbulence and chaos as the Austro-Hungarian Empire dissolved and war and revolution raged. Until the early

1930s, German universities and research institutions attracted many future Nobel laureates from Central Europe. A number of Western Europeans went to Cambridge or Oxford instead.

Hitler's appointment as Chancellor in 1933, the persecution of the Jews in the 1930s and the outbreak of World War Two shifted the scientific – and much of the cultural – focus from Europe to the United States. Leading artists, writers and scientists were among the 400,000 people who left Europe by compulsion or choice. Europe suffered a brain drain, while the United States benefited from an intellectual influx that made a considerable contribution to its post-war scientific and economic upturn.

12.7 Can the settings of creativity be designed?

Is it possible to plan and design settings that favour creative processes? If so, what is required? One answer supported by this book is that many prerequisites for creativity can be designed but that the results do not generally manifest until much later on. Most settings discussed by this book share certain requirements when it comes to creativity. However, other criteria are specific to particular places and small groups of individuals, along with their experiences and contact networks. Just because a group of phenomena appear together in a particular environment does not mean that there is a cause–effect relationship between them. A set of circumstances that appear to be propitious in one place may not have the same impact somewhere else. Such correlations are complex and insufficiently known. Chance and coincidence may play a significant role.

While it is difficult to consciously create settings that nurture innovative processes, it is easy to unconsciously block them or bridle those that are already under way. For instance, rules and other measures may have the well-intentioned purpose of rapidly boosting oversight and productivity. Skill, diversity, variation, communication and mobility are the most reliable building blocks of creativity. When they are hedged in and circumscribed by restrictions, the risk of stagnation and decline rears its ugly head. Thus, a reasonable, concise conclusion from the material presented by this book is as follows: Both historically and in the contemporary world, places where creative people gather, accumulate resources and enjoy manoeuvrability offer the most promising opportunities for thoroughgoing innovation and development.

Proceeding from that conclusion, planning for the purpose of ensuring innovation clearly has the best prospects of success if devoted to the development and preservation of milieux that attract pioneers and entrepreneurs. The impetus for such migration has been unusually strong in periods of political upheaval and those in which the availability of economic resources has varied widely among geographic areas and places. Whether private or public, planning that is able to shape institutional arrangements, the labour market, living conditions and the allocation of economic resources is among the comprehensive measures that favour long-term development. The next section examines several questions that highlight the difficulties associated with planning in detail for creative processes.

12.8   Dichotomies of creativity

Dichotomy refers to division into two mutually exclusive entities. The word, which comes from the Greek roots for 'two' and 'cut', is used differently depending on the scientific discipline. A logical dichotomy refers to two mutually exclusive concepts. A dichotomous variable, for instance gender, in the social sciences represents a characteristic for which there are two mutually exclusive categories.

This book uses certain pairs of concepts that are ostensibly opposed to each other. Some of them appear in Figure 12.1. But they are not dichotomies, at least in the true sense of the word. While they entail certain contrasts, they are far from mutually exclusive. The book points instead to the interplay of oppositions and connections that generate dynamic force fields. The complex relationships that influence creative processes often emerge from such fields. Additional comments are needed to illustrate how these pairs of opposites interact.

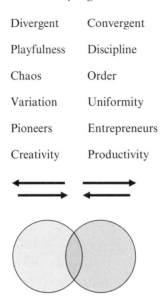

Figure 12.1 Pairs of opposites and contrasts that generate dynamic force fields

The first pair consists of divergent and convergent thinking. Divergent thinking is the ability to identify solutions that challenge conventional wisdom. A truly creative person can break loose from generally accepted patterns of thought, tear down walls and embark on new paths. In order to do so, the person must ordinarily possess thorough knowledge of the old paths and the obstacles that stand in the way of fresh thinking.

The intersection of two spheres of thought (circles in the diagram) illustrates such a relationship. How much the circles overlap varies between pairs of concepts and individuals. Young children or people with certain mental disorders may experience the left side independent of the right side. The opposite may be true among highly educated people with advanced specialist training. Based on the material in this book, a reasonable hypothesis is that the areas of intersection energize the dynamic force fields in which creativity – in the long run successful – arises.

Tension and interaction between playfulness and discipline is particularly relevant in scientific fields. Research is largely playful in nature, while constrained by a specific type of discipline. You might describe research as imagination that is amenable to testing. But without imagination and fantasy there will be nothing to test. As the Nobel laureate in chemistry Ilya Prigogine said about the relationship between chaos and order, chance and organization:

> Perfect order is crystalline death; total chaos is formless death. Between them is a fantastic cross-fertilisation of perspective and surprise on which creativity is based. That is the source of all potential.

Various geographic and institutional settings have given rise to observations about the obstacles to, and incentives for, creative processes. Variation and diversity favour such processes, whereas uniformity and homogeneity inhibit them. An unstable and ostensibly chaotic setting can provide truly creative people with the manoeuvrability they need to shake off convention and ingrained ways of thinking. A well-planned setting hemmed in by rigid regulations may allow for many good functional characteristics while restraining innovative forces in an unwanted manner.

Well-intentioned prioritization of qualities associated with the words on the right side of Figure 12.1 is easy and common. Examining and promoting qualities associated with the words on the left side is rarer and more difficult. There are two obvious reasons for that distinction – prevailing social assumptions, and the ability to observe and measure. Economic growth is generally viewed as a pillar of general welfare. Particularly in a capitalist economy, entrepreneurs play a vital role as risk-takers, founders of new businesses and champions of innovative processes. A central observation of this book is that entrepreneurs are many in number, rewarded by their surroundings and active in the scientific and artistic world as well as business. Many organizations rely on steady productivity growth that is visible and measurable in terms of the relationship between output and invested resources. Such considerations are fundamental to their assessments of success and quality.

Pioneers are creative in the restrictive, profound sense of the word. Their contributions are the ultimate source of innovation and development. Frequently their work is not acknowledged until much later on. There are few of them, and their contemporaries are rarely in a position to fully recognize and gauge their accomplishments. Thus, comprehensive innovative processes originate in the interplay of pioneers and entrepreneurs.

Without pioneers, entrepreneurs would not have anything new to bring to the market. Without entrepreneurs, the efforts of pioneers may never become a successful innovation. A single person may occasionally possess qualities associated with both pioneers and entrepreneurs. More often, progress flows from their mutual interaction in both time and space.

Notes

Chapter 1

1. Dean, Keith (2006) 'Creativity around the world in 80 ways . . . but with one Destination', in James Kaufman and Robert Sternberg (eds), *The International Handbook of Creativity*, New York: Cambridge University Press, p. 490.
2. Mouchiroud, Christophe and Todd Lubart (2006) 'Past, present, and future perspectives on creativity in France and French-Speaking Switzerland', in James Kaufman and Robert Sternberg (eds), *The International Handbook of Creativity*, New York: Cambridge University Press.
3. Heilbron, John (1992), 'Creativity and big science', *Physics Today*, November 1992.
4. A free translation from Swedish. Burton, Nina (2002), *Det som muser viskat. Sju frågor och hundra svar om skapande och kreativitet*, Stockholm/Stehag: Brutus Östlings Bokförlag Symposion, pp. 25–26.
5. For some alternatives see Kaufman, James and Robert Sternberg (eds), *The International Handbook of Creativity*, New York: Cambridge University Press.
6. Törnqvist, Gunnar (2004), *Kreativitetens geografi*, Stockholm: SNS Förlag.
7. See Sahlin, Nils-Eric (2001), *Kreativitetens filosofi*, Nora: Nya Doxa.

Chapter 2

1. A number of his early reports are summarized in Guilford, Joy Paul (1967), *The Nature of Human Intelligence*, New York: McGraw-Hill. See Sahlin, Nils-Eric (2001), *Kreativitetens filosofi*. Nora: Nya Doxa, p. 92.

2. Koestler, Arthur (1964), *The Act of Creation*, London: Hutchinson & Co.
3. Ibid. p. 86.
4. The version of the story presented here was largely taken from ibid. p. 105 ff. It also appears in many other places, including a number of dictionaries and encyclopaedias.
5. Ibid. p. 123.
6. De Bono has written 75 books since the mid 1960s. They have been translated into 37 languages. For instance, see (1970), *Lateral Thinking: Creativity Step by Step*, New York: Harper & Row; (1985), *Six Thinking Hats*, New York: Brown & Co.; (1984), *Tänk kreativt*, Stockholm: Brombergs.
7. Wallas, Graham (1926), *The Art of Thought*, New York: Harcourt Brace.
8. Koestler, Arthur, op. cit., p. 178 ff.

Chapter 3

1. See Torrence, E.P. (1962), *Guiding Creative Talent*, Englewood Cliffs, NJ: Prentice Hall; (1974), *The Torrence Test of Creative Thinking*, Bensenville: Scholastic Testing Service; Smith, Gudmund and Carlsson, Ingegerd (1990), 'The creative process: a functional model based on empirical studies from early childhood to middle age', *Psychological Issues, Monograph 57*, New York: International Universities Press.
2. See Smith, Gudmund and Ingegerd Carlsson (1990), 'The creative process: a functional model based on empirical studies from early childhood to middle age', *Psychological Issues, Monograph 57*, New York: International Universities Press.
3. Richard Florida (2001), *The Rise of the Creative Class. And how it's Transforming Work, Leisure, Community and Everyday Life*, New York: Basic Books.
4. The statement appears in an unpublished document that was put together when preparing the centennial of the Nobel Prize.

5. Sahlin, Nils-Eric (2001), *Kreativitetens filosofi*, Nora: Nya Doxa, pp. 93; 145–6.
6. Collins, Randall (1998), *The Sociology of Philosophies. A Global Theory of Intellectual Change*, Cambridge, MA and London: Harvard University Press, p. 58.
7. Weisberg, Robert W. (1993), *Beyond the Myth of Genius*, New York: Freeman.
8. Schumpeter, Joseph (1939), *Business Cycles: A Theoretical, Historical, and Statistical Analysis of the Capitalist Process*, New York: McGraw-Hill; (1942), *Capitalism, Socialism and Democracy*, New York: Harper & Brothers.
9. See interview with Gudmund Smith in Hansson, Bengt (2006), 'Låt kreativiteten växa i lagom stora miljöer', editorial in *Tvärsnitt* 4/06, Tidskrift för humanistisk och samhällsvetenskaplig forskning, Stockholm: Swedish Research Council.

Chapter 4

1. Many of the descriptions were presented previously in Andersson, Åke E., Gunnar Törnqvist, Folke Snickars and Öberg Sture (1984), *Regional mångfald till rikets gagn. En idébok från ERU*, Stockholm: Liber Förlag; Ambjörnsson, Ronny (ed.) (1986), *Från Aten till Los Angeles. Idéhistoriska miljöer*, Malmö: Liber Hermods; Larsson, Ulf (ed.) (2001), *Cultures of Creativity: the Centennial Exhibition of the Nobel Prize*, Canton MA: Science History Publications/USA.
    See also Törnqvist, Gunnar (1983), 'Kreativitetens geografi', *Svensk Geografisk Årsbok*, Lund: Gleerup; (1989), 'La Créativité: Une Perspective Géographique', *La Géographie de la Créativité et de l'Innovation*, Paris: Université de Paris-Sorbonne; (1990), 'Towards a geography of creativity', in Shachar, Ari and Öberg Sture (eds), *The World Economy and the Spatial Organization of Power*, Aldershot: Avebury.
2. Janik, Allan and Stephen Toulmin (1973), *Wittgenstein's Vienna*, New York: Simon and Schuster.
3. See note 4.

4. Beach, Sylvia (2008), *Shakespeare and Company*, Lund: Ellerströms fölag.
5. Extensive documentation is available in Bradbury, Malcolm (ed.) (1996), *The Atlas of Literature*, London: De Agostini Editions.
6. Castells, Manuel (1996), *The Rise of the Network Society, Volume I The Information Age: Economy, Society and Culture*, Oxford: Blackwell Publishers.
7. Hall, Peter and Pascal Preston (1988), *The Carrier Wave: New Information Technology and the Geography of Innovation, 1846–2003*, London: Unwin Hyman.
8. The concept is used and further developed in Andersson, Åke E., Gunnar Törnqvist, Sture Öberg and Snickars Folke (1984), *Regional mångfald till rikets gagn. En idébok från ERU*, Stockholm: Liber Förlag.
9. Burton, Nina (2002), *Det som muser viskat. Sju frågor och hundra svar om skapande och kreativitet*, Stockholm/Stehag: Brutus Östlings Bokförlag Symposion, p. 33.

Chapter 5

1. Hall, Peter (1998), *Cities in Civilization. Culture, Innovation, and Urban Order*, London: Weidenfeld & Nicolson. The quote and questions are on the cover.
2. Andersson, Åke E. (1985), *Kreativitet. StorStadens Framtid*, Stockholm: Prisma; Andersson, Åke E. and Strömquist, Ulf (1988), *K-Samhällets Framtid*, Stockholm: Prisma.
3. Landry, Charles (2000), *The Creative City: A Toolkit for Urban Innovators*, London: Earthscan Publications.
4. Cederlund, Kerstin (2004), *Universitetet, kulturen och staden*, Stockholm: SNS Förlag.
5. For a more detailed presentation of the concept of escalator region, see Wikhall, Maria (2001), *Universiteten och kompetenslandskapet. Effekter av den högre utbildningens tillväxt och regionala spridning i Sverige*, Lund: Institutionen för kulturgeografi och ekonomisk geografi, Lunds universitet, 218.
6. Florida, Richard (2001), *The Rise of the Creative Class:*

And how it's Transforming Work, Leisure, Community and Everyday Life, New York: Basic Books, p. 6.

7. Cf. ibid. pp. 68–9.

8. Information taken from Saxenian, AnnaLee (1999), *Silicon Valley's New Immigrant Entrepreneurs*, Berkeley: Public Policy Institute of California.

9. See Porter, Michael (1990), *The Competitive Advantage of Nations*, London and Basingstoke: The Macmillan Press.

10. Storper, Michael (1989), 'The Transition to Flexible Specialisation in the U.S. Film Industry: External Economies, the Division of Labor, and Crossing Industrial Divides', *Cambridge Journal of Economics*, **13**.

11. For these figures see Barley, Stephen (1996), *The New World of Work*, London: British North American Committee.

12. Oldenburg, Ray (1989), *The Great Good Place. Cafes, Coffee Shops, Bars, Hair Salons and Other Hangouts at the Heart of a Community*, New York: Marlowe and Company.

13. Schultz, Theodore W. (1971), *Investment in Human Capital: The Role of Education and Research*, London: Free Press.

14. For a more detailed definition of the concepts, see Bourdieu, Pierre and Louis Wacquant (1992), *An Invitation to Reflexive Sociology*, Chicago: University of Chicago Press; Coleman, James (1990), *Foundations of Social Theory*, Cambridge, MA: Harvard University Press; Westlund, Hans and Roger Bolton (2003), 'Local Social Capital and Entrepreneurship', *Small Business Economics*, **21**.

15. Putnam, Robert (1993), *Making Democracy Work: Civic Traditions in Modern Italy*, Princeton: Princeton University Press.

16. The 'First Italy' covers the early industrialized areas of the north-west, the 'Second Italy' covers the under-developed agricultural areas of the south. The designations derive from Bagnasco, Arnaldo (1977), *Tre*

Italie. La problematica territoriale dello sviluppo italiano, Bologna: Il Mulino.

17. Florida, Richard (2001), cf. ibid., pp. 267–82; Jacobs, Jane (1961), *The Death and Life of Great American Cities*, New York: Random House; (1984), *Cities and the Wealth of Nations*, Harmondsworth: Penguin Books.

18. Hansen, Høgni Kalsø (2008), *The Urban Turn – and the Location of Economic Activities*, Lund: Lund University. The thesis consists of five papers written together with others. Hansen summarizes the papers in an introductory chapter.

19. See North, Douglass (1990), *Institutions, Institutional Change and Economic Performance*, New York: Cambridge University Press.

Chapter 6

1. Efficiency and productivity refer to the ratio of output to input. Output may be production per unit of time in the case of a business and graduation figures or the number of scientific publications in the case of a university.

2. Among the extensive literature, see Thomson, W. (1965), "'Bureaucracy and Innovation'", *Administrative Science Quarterly*, **10** (1), 1965; Ekvall, Göran *et al.* (1987), *Organisation och innovation: en studie av fyra divisioner vid EKA Kemi i Bohus*, Lund: Studentlitteratur; Kanter, Rosabeth Moss (1999), *The Change Masters. Corporate Entrepreneurs at Work*, London: International Thomson Business Press.

3. http://en.wikipedia.org/wiki/Nokia; Sörlin, Sverker and Gunnar Törnqvist (2006), 'Universitet och regioner – ett återbesök', in Blückert, Kjell and Eva Österberg (eds), *Gränslöst – forskning i Sverige och i världen, Festskift till Dan Brändström*. Stockholm: Natur och Kultur.

4. See note 19 of Chapter 5.

5. Burton, Nina (2002), *Det som muser viskat. Sju frågor och hundra svar om skapande och kreativitet*, Stockholm/

Stehag: Brutus Östlings Bokförlag Symposion, pp. 41–2.

Chapter 7

1. Castells, Manuel (1996), *The Rise of the Network Society. The Information Age: Economy, Society and Culture, Volume I*, Oxford: Blackwell Publishers.
2. Rosenberg, Nathan and L.E. Birdzell (1986), *How the West Grew Rich: The Economic Transformation of the Industrial World*, New York: Basic Books.
3. Gibbons, Michael (1994), *The New Production of Knowledge. The Dynamics of Science and Research in Contemporary Societies*, London: Sage Publications.
4. The research reports that will be summarized are presented in the following works: Castells, Manuel and Hall, Peter (1994), *Technopoles of the World: The Making of 21st-Century Industrial Complexes*, London: Routledge; Decoster, Elisabeth and Muriel Taberies (1986), *L'Innovation dans un Pôle Scientifique et Technologie: Le Cas de la Cité Scientifique Ile de France Sud*, Paris: Université Paris 1; Hall, Peter (1997), 'The university and the city', *GeoJournal*, **41** (4); Hall, Peter, Michael Breheny, Randy McQuaid and Hart, Douglas. (1987), *Western Sunrise: The Genesis and Growth of Britain's Major High-Tech Corridor*, London: Allen and Unwin; Keeble, David (1989), 'High-technology industry and regional development in Britain: the case of the Cambridge phenomenon', *Environment and Planning C*, 153–72; Saxenian, AnnLee (1994), *Regional Advantage: Culture and Competition in Silicon Valley and Route 128*, Cambridge, MA: Harvard University Press; Scott, Allan (1993), *Technopolis: High-Technology Industry and Regional Development in Southern California*, Berkeley, CA: University of California Press; Tatsuno, S.M. (1986), *The Technopolis Strategy: Japan, High Technology, and the Control of the Twenty-first Century*, New York: Prentice-Hall Press.
5. Sörlin, Sverker and Gunnar Törnqvist (2000), *Kunskap*

för välstånd. Universiteten och omvandlingen av Sverige.
Stockholm: SNS Förlag.

6. See Charles Edquist's article, 'Systems of innovation
    approaches – their emergence and characteristics',
    in Charles Edquist (ed.) (1997), *Systems of Innovation:
    Technologies, Institutions, and Organizations*, London
    and Washington DC: Pinter. The article and rest
    of the book contain a thorough review of relevant
    literature.

7. Porter, Michael (1990), *The Competitive Advantage of
    Nations.* New York: Simon & Schuster; Porter, Michael
    (1998), 'Clusters and the new economics of competi-
    tion', *Harvard Business Review*, November–December.

8. Perroux, François (1955), 'Note sur la notion de "pôle
    de croissance"', *Économie Appliquée*, **8**.

9. Malmberg, Anders, Örjan Sölvell and Ivo Sander
    (1996), 'Spatial clustering, local accumulation of knowl-
    edge and firm competitiveness', *Geografisk Annaler*,
    78B, No. 2; Tson Söderström, Hans (ed.) (2001), *Kluster.
    se Sverige i den nya ekonomiska geografin*, Stockholm: SNS
    Förlag.

10. Cooke, Philip (1992), 'Regional innovations systems.
    Competitive regulation in the New Europe', *Geoforum,*
    23; Asheim, Björn Terje (1995), 'Regionale innovasjons-
    system. En sosialt og territorielt forankret teknolo-
    gipolitik', *Nordisk samhällsgeografisk tidskrift*, **20**;
    Fagerberg, Jan (ed.) (2004), *The Oxford Handbook of
    Innovation*, Oxford: Oxford University Press.

Chapter 8

1. *Universiteten och forskningen – en vision. Utmaningar
    och problem.* Forskningsstrategiska utskottet, Kungl.
    Vetenskapsakademien, 2008.

2. See http://scientific.thomsonreuters.com.

3. A free translation from Swedish. Österberg, Eva (2008),
    'Universitet är inget företag', *Sydsvenskan*, 6 April.
    A longer version of the text appears in *Universitetets
    frihet*, Kulturforum vid Lunds universitet.

4. For an overview and additional examples, see Forneng, Stig, Ingemar Lind and Thorsten Nybom (2007), *En svensk universitetsranking – 2007*, Stockholm: Universitets- och högskoleämbetet.
5. Academic Ranking of World Universities: http:// ed.sjtu.edu.en/rank/2007; Times Higher Education (THE): http://topuniversities.com/home/; The Ranking: Leiden, http://www.cwts.nl/cwts/LR.

Chapter 9

1. Kerstin Cederlund (1999), *Universitet. Platser där världar möts*, Stockholm: SNS Förlag.
2. Törnqvist, Gunnar (2002), *Science at the Cutting Edge. The Future of the Øresund Region*, Copenhagen: Copenhagen Business School Press.
3. See the catalogue that was put together for the 2001 Centennial Exhibition of the Nobel Prize. Larsson, Ulf (ed.) (2001), *Cultures of Creativity: the Centennial Exhibition of the Nobel Prize*, Canton, MA: Science History Publications/USA. Unless another source is cited, the descriptions of the various settings are based on this catalogue.
4. All of these Nobel laureates were associated with Cambridge at one time or another, but most of them were employed somewhere else when they were awarded the prize (see Chapter 10).
5. Hollingsworth, Rogers and Ellen Jane Hollingsworth (2003), 'Stora upptäckter och biomedicinska forskningsorganisationer', Kim, Lillemor and Mårtens, Pehr (eds), *Den vildväxande högskolan. Studier av reformer, miljöer och kunskapsvägar*, SISTER, Skrifter 8, Nora: Bokförlaget Nya Doxa.
6. Barabási, Albert-László (2005), 'Network theory – the emergence of the creative'; Guimerà, Roger, Uzzi, Brian, Spiro, Jarrett and Nunes Amaral, Luis (2005), 'Team assembly mechanisms determine collaboration network structure and team performance'. Both articles appeared in *Science*, **308**, April 2005.

7. These kinds of data may be obtained from *Web of Science*. See Chapter 8, note 2.

8. See Cederlund, Kerstin (1999), *Universitet – Platser där världar möts*, Stockholm: SNS Förlag.

9. For a detailed discussion, see Törnqvist, Gunnar (1998), *Renässans för regioner. Om tekniken och den sociala kommunikationens villkor*, Stockholm: SNS Förlag; Törnqvist, Gunnar (2004), 'Creativity in time and space', *Geografiska Annaler*, 86 B.

10. Hollingsworth, Rogers and Hollingsworth, Ellen Jane (2003), cf. ibid.

11. Sahlin, Nils-Eric (2001), *Kreativitetens filosofi*, Nora: Nya Doxa.

12. Hansson, Bengt (2006), 'Låt kreativiteten växa i lagom stora miljöer', *Tvärsnitt*, **4** (6).

13. *Universiteten och forskningen – en vision. Utmaningar och problem.* Forskningsstrategiska utskottet, Royal Swedish Academy of Sciences, 2008.

14. Sahlin, Nils-Eric (2001), cf. ibid. pp. 162–3.

15. Hollingsworth, Rogers and Ellen Jane Hollingsworth (2003), cf. ibid, p. 248.

16. Pääbo, Svante (2007), 'Byggnaden ska gynna ett socialt liv', *Kreativa rum*, **2**.

17. Hägerstrand, Torsten (1985), 'Universiteten som kreativ miljö', in Ström, G. (ed), *Erövra universiteten åter*, Stockholm: Liber.

Chapter 10

1. www.nobelprize.org.

2. The presentation is based primarily on personal experience with the ninth class of the Academy.

3. www.nobelprize.org.

4. Only the basic principles of, and a few observations about, ongoing research will be taken up. A more comprehensive approach is not feasible within the constraints of this book. Much of the material and its wealth of detail were presented in a doctoral thesis after its use by the centennial exhibition. See Thufvesson, Ola

(2006), *Kreativitetens yttre villkor. Miljöer, rörlighet och nobelpristagare*, Lund: Institutionen för kulturgeografi och ekonomisk geografi.

5. Hargittai, István (2002), *The Road to Stockholm. Nobel Prizes, Science, and Scientists*, Oxford: Oxford University Press.

6. Lindqvist, Svante (2006), 'The R&D Production Model: A Brueg(h)elesque Alternative', in Guy Neave, Kjell Blückert and Torsten Nybom, *European Research University. An Historical Parenthesis?*, New York: Palgrave Macmillan.
The percentages on which the various bars are based have been rounded off.

7. www.nobel.se

8. Thufvesson, Ola (2006), *Kreativitetens yttre villkor. Miljöer, rörlighet och nobelpristagare*, Lund: Institutionen för kulturgeografi och ekonomisk geografi, pp. 125–9.

Chapter 11

1. Personal letter of 23 March 2004 following the widespread claim that time–space geography had emerged in the 1960s.

2. A number of works by Hägerstrand, as well as doctoral theses and geographic manuals, describe the basic principles of time–space geography. Two of the earliest is Hägerstrand, Torsten (1970), 'Tidsanvändning och omgivningsstruktur', *SOU*, **14** and (1970), 'What about People in Regional Science?', *Regional Science Association Papers*, **XXIV**, pp. 7–21.
A comprehensive presentation of Hägerstrand's works and thinking appears in Carlestam, Gösta and Barbro Sollbe (eds) (1991), *Om tidens vidd och tingens ordning. Texter av Torsten Hägerstrand*, Stockholm: Statens råd för byggnadsforskning.

3. See Wikhall, Maria (2001), *Universiteten och kompetenslandskapet. Effekter av den högre utbildningens tillväxt och regionala spridning i Sverige*, Lund: Institutionen för kulturgeografi och ekonomisk geografi, Lunds universitet.

4. Hargittai, István (2002), *The Road to Stockholm. Nobel Prizes, Science and Scientists*, Oxford: Oxford University Press.
5. Quotes taken from Marx, George, *Provision for a Long Journey*, unpublished manuscript, Department of Atomic Physics, Eötvös University, Budapest.
6. Marx, George (1998), *Conflicts and Creativity – The Hungarian Lesson*, lecture at the Royal Swedish Academy of Sciences, 14 October.
7. *Ibid.*
8. *Ibid.*
9. *Ibid.*

References

Ambjörnsson, Ronny (ed.) (1986), *Från Aten till Los Angeles. Idéhistoriska miljöer*, Malmö: Liber Hermods.

Andersson, Åke E. (1985), *Kreativitet. StorStadens Framtid*, Stockholm: Prisma.

Andersson, Åke E., Gunnar Törnqvist, Sture Öberg and Folke Snickars (1984), *Regional mångfald till rikets gagn. En idébok från ERU*, Stockholm: Liber Förlag.

Andersson, Åke E. and Ulf Strömquist (1988), *K-Samhällets Framtid*, Stockholm: Prisma.

Asheim, Björn Terje (1995), 'Regionale innovasjonssystem. En sosialt og territorielt forankret teknologipolitik', *Nordisk samhällsgeografisk tidskrift*, **20**.

Bagnasco, Arnaldo (1977), *Tre Italie. La problematica territoriale dello sviluppo italiano*, Bologna: Il Mulino.

Barabási, Albert-László (2005), 'Network theory – the emergence of the creative enterprise', *Science*, **308**, April 2005.

Barley, Stephen (1996), *The New World of Work*, London: British North American Committee.

Beach, Sylvia (2008), *Shakespeare and Company*, Lund: Ellerströms förlag.

Blückert, Kjell and Eva Österberg (2006), *Gränslöst*

– *forskning i Sverige och i världen. Festskift till Dan Brändström*, Stockholm: Natur och Kultur.

Bourdieu, Pierre and Louis Wacquant (1992), *An Invitation to Reflexive Sociology*, Chicago: University of Chicago Press.

Bradbury, Malcolm (ed.) (1996), *The Atlas of Literature*, London: De Agostini Editions.

Burton, Nina (2002), *Det som muser viskat. Sju frågor och hundra svar om skapande och kreativitet*, Stockholm/Stehag: Brutus Östlings Bokförlag Symposion.

Buttimer, Anne (ed.) (1983), *Creativity and Context: A Seminar Report*, Lund Studies of Geography, B Human Geography, No. 50. Lund: Gleerup.

Carlestam, Gösta and Barbro Sollbe (eds) (1991), *Om tidens vidd och tingens ordning. Texter av Torsten Hägerstrand*, Stockholm: Statens råd för byggnadsforskning.

Castells, Manuel (1996), *The Rise of the Network Society, The Information Age: Economy, Society and Culture, Volume I*, Oxford: Blackwell Publishers.

Castells, Manuel and Peter Hall (1994), *Technopoles of the World: The Making of 21st-Century Industrial Complexes*, London: Routledge.

Cederlund, Kerstin (1999), *Universitet. Platser där världar möts*, Stockholm: SNS Förlag.

Cederlund, Kerstin (2004), *Universitetet, kulturen och staden*, Stockholm: SNS Förlag.

Coleman, James (1990), *Foundations of Social Theory*, Cambridge, MA: Harvard University Press.

Collins, Randall (1998), *The Sociology of*

Philosophies. A Global Theory of Intellectual Change, Cambridge, MA and London: Harvard University Press.

Cooke, Philip (1992), 'Regional innovations systems. Competitive regulation in the New Europe', *Geoforum*, **23**.

de Bono, Edward (1970), *Lateral Thinking: Creativity Step by Step*, New York: Harper & Row.

de Bono, Edward (1984), *Tänk kreativt*, Stockholm: Brombergs.

de Bono, Edward (1985), *Six Thinking Hats*, New York: Brown & Co.

Decoster, Elisabeth and Muriel Taberies (1986), *L'Innovation dans un Pôle Scientifique et Technologie: Le Cas de la Cité Scientifique Ile de France Sud*, Paris: Université Paris 1.

Edquist, Charles (1997), 'Systems of innovation approaches – their emergence and characteristics', in Charles Edquist (ed.), *Systems of Innovation: Technologies, Institutions, and Organizations*, London and Washington DC: Pinter.

Edquist, Charles (ed.) (1997), *Systems of Innovation: Technologies, Institutions, and Organizations*, London and Washington DC: Pinter.

Ekvall, Göran et al. (1987), *Organisation och innovation: en studie av fyra divisioner vid EKA Kemi i Bohus*, Lund: Studentlitteratur.

Fagerberg, Jan, David Mowery and Richard R. Nelson (eds) (2004), *The Oxford Handbook of Innovation*, Oxford: Oxford University Press.

Florida, Richard (2001), *The Rise of the Creative*

Class: And how it´s Transforming Work, Leisure, Community and Everyday Life, New York: Basic Books.

Florida, Richard (2001), *Den kreativa klassens framväxt*, Göteborg: Daidalos.

Forneng, Stig, Ingemar Lind and Thorsten Nybom (2007), *En svensk Universitetsranking – 2007*, Stockholm: Universitets- och högskoleämbetet.

Gibbons, Michael (1994), *The New Production of Knowledge. The Dynamics of Science and Research in Contemporary Societies*, London: Sage Publications.

Guilford, Joy Paul (1967), *The Nature of Human Intelligence*, New York: McGraw-Hill.

Guimerà, Roger, Brian Uzzi, Jarrett Spiro and Luis Nunes Amaral (2005), 'Team assembly mechanisms determine collaboration network structure and team performance', *Science*, **308**, April 2005.

Gustafsson, Lars, Susan Howar and Lars Niklasson (eds) (1993), *The Creative Process*, Stockholm: Swedish Ministry of Education and Science.

Hägerstrand, Torsten (1970), 'What about people in regional science', *Regional Science Association Papers*, **XXIV**, 7–21.

Hägerstrand, Torsten (1970), 'Tidsanvändning och omgivningsstruktur', *SOU*, **14**.

Hägerstrand, Torsten (1985), 'Universiteten som kreativ miljö', in Ström, G (ed.), *Erövra universiteten åter*, Stockholm: Liber.

Hall, Peter (1997), 'The university and the city', *GeoJournal*, **41**(4).

Hall, Peter (1998), *Cities in Civilization. Culture, Innovation, and Urban Order*, London: Weidenfeld & Nicolson.

Hall, Peter, Michael Breheny, Ronald McQuaid and Douglas Hart (1987), *Western Sunrise: The Genesis and Growth of Britain's Major High-Tech Corridor*, London: Allen and Unwin.

Hall, Peter and Pascal Preston (1988), *The Carrier Wave: New Information Technology and the Geography of Innovation, 1846–2003*, London: Unwin Hyman.

Hallencreutz, Daniel, Per Lundequist and Anders Malmberg (2007), *Populärmusik från Svedala. Näringspolitiska lärdomar av det Svenska musikklustrets framväxt*, Stockholm: SNS Förlag.

Hansen, Høgni Kalsø (2008), *The Urban Turn – and the Location of Economic Activities*, Lund: Lund University.

Hansson, Bengt (2006), 'Låt kreativiteten växa i lagom stora miljöer', leading article in *Tvärsnitt* 4/06.

Hargittai, István (2002), *The Road to Stockholm. Nobel Prizes, Science, and Scientists*, Oxford: Oxford University Press.

Heilbron, John (1992), 'Creativity and Big Science', *Physics Today*, November 1992.

Hollingsworth, Rogers and Ellen Jane Hollingsworth (2003), 'Stora upptäckter och biomedicinska forsknings-organisationer', in Lillemor Kim and Pehr Mårtens (eds), *Den vildväxande högskolan. Studier av reformer, miljöer och kunskapsvägar*, SISTER, Skrifter 8. Nora: Bokförlaget Nya Doxa.

200   *The geography of creativity*

I framtidens kölvatten: Samhällskonflikter 25 år framåt. Rapport från FA-rådet. Stockholm: Publica, 1986.

Jacobs, Jane (1961), *The Death and Life of Great American Cities*, New York: Random House.

Jacobs, Jane (1984), *Cities and the Wealth of Nations*, Harmondsworth: Penguin Books.

Janik, Allan and Stephen Toulmin (1973), *Wittgenstein's Vienna*, New York: Simon and Schuster.

Jönsson, Christer, Sven Tägil and Gunnar Törnqvist (2006), *Organizing European Space*, London: Sage Publications.

Jönsson, Christer, Sven Tägil and Gunnar Törnqvist (2007), *Europa quo vadis? Integration och splittring i tid och rum*, Stockholm: SNS Förlag.

Kanter, Rosabeth Moss (1999), *The Change Masters. Corporate Entrepreneurs at Work*, London: International Thomson Business Press.

Kaufman, James and Robert Sternberg (eds) (2006), *The International Handbook of Creativity*, New York: Cambridge University Press.

Keeble, David (1989), 'High-technology industry and regional development in Britain: the case of the Cambridge phenomenon', *Environment and Planning C*, 153–72.

Kim, Lillemor and Pehr Mårtens (eds), *Den vildväxande högskolan. Studier av reformer, miljöer och kunskapsvägar.* SISTER, Skrifter 8. Nora: Bokförlaget Nya Doxa.

Klein, Georg (ed.) (1990), *Om krativitet och flow*, Stockholm: Brombergs.

Koestler, Arthur (1964), *The Act of Creation*, London: Hutchinson & Co.

Koestler, Arthur (1982), *Janus En sammanfattning*, Göteborg: Bokförlaget Korpen.

Landry, Charles (2000), *The Creative City. A Toolkit for Urban Innovators*, London: Earthscan Publications.

Larsson, Ulf (ed.) (2001), *Människor miljöer och kreativitet. Nobelpriset 100 år*, Stockholm: Atlantis och Nobelmuseet.

Larsson, Ulf (ed.) (2001), *Cultures of Creativity: the Centennial Exhibition of the Nobel Prize*, Canton, MA: Science History Publications/USA.

Lindqvist, Svante (2006), 'The R&D production model: a Brueg(h)elesque alternative' in Guy Neave, Kjell Blückert and Torsten Nybom (eds), *European Research University. A Historical Parenthesis?*, New York: Palgrave Macmillan.

Lövtrup, Michael (2004), 'Mix av personlighetstyper bäst för kreativiteten i forskarmiljöer', *Tvärsnitt* **4** (04), Tidskrift för humanistisk och samhällsvetenskaplig forskning. Stockholm: Vetenskapsrådet.

Malmberg, Anders, Örjan Sölvell and Ivo Sander (1996), 'Spatial clustering, local accumulation of knowledge and firm competitiveness', *Geografiska Annaler*, **78B**(2).

Marx, George (1998), *Provision for a Long Journey*, unpublished manuscript, Department of Atomic Physics, Eötvös University, Budapest.

Marx, George (1998), 'Conflicts and Creativity – The Hungarian Lesson', lecture at the Royal Swedish Academy of Sciences, 14 October.

Mouchiroud, Christophe and Todd Lubart (2006), 'Past, present, and future perspectives on creativity in France and French-speaking Switzerland', in James Kaufman and Robert Sternberg (eds), *The International Handbook of Creativity*, New York: Cambridge University Press.

Neave, Guy, Kjell Blückert and Torsten Nybom (eds) (2006), *European Research University. An Historical Parenthesis?*, New York: Palgrave Macmillan.

North, Douglass (1990), *Institutions, Institutional Change and Economic Performance*, New York: Cambridge University Press.

Oldenburg, Ray (1989), *The Great Good Place. Cafes, Coffee Shops, Bars, Hair Salons and Other Hangouts at the Heart of a Community*, New York: Marlowe and Company.

Österberg, Eva (2008), 'Universitet är inget företag', *Sydsvenskan*, 6 April.

Pääbo, Svante (2007), 'Byggnaden ska gynna ett socialt liv', *Kreativa rum*, 2.

Perroux, François (1955), 'Note sur la notion de "pôle de croissance"', *ÉconomieAppliquée*, 8.

Porter, Michael (1990), *The Competitive Advantage of Nations*, London and Basingstoke: The Macmillan Press.

Porter, Michael (1998), 'Clusters and the new economics of competition', *Harvard Business Review*, November–December.

Prigogine, Ilya (1993), 'Creativity in the sciences and the humanities. A study in the relation between the two cultures', in Lars Gustafsson, Susan Howar and Lars Niklasson (eds), *The Creative Process*, Stockholm: Swedish Ministry of Education and Science.

Putnam, Robert (1993), *Making Democracy Work: Civic Traditions in Modern Italy*, Princeton: Princeton University Press.

Putnam, Robert (1996), *Den fungerande demokratin. Medborgarandans rötter i Italien*, Stockholm: SNS Förlag.

Rose, Joanna (1996), 'Receptet på framgång', *Forskning och Framsteg*, **8**.

Rosenberg, Nathan and L.E. Birdzell Jr (1986), *How the West Grew Rich: The Economic Transformation of the Industrial World*, New York: Basic Books.

Rosenberg, Nathan and L.E. Birdzell Jr (1991), *Västvärldens väg till välstånd*, Stockholm: SNS Förlag.

Sahlin, Nils-Eric (2001), *Kreativitetens filosofi*, Nora: Nya Doxa.

Saxenian, AnnLee (1994), *Regional Advantage: Culture and Competition in Silicon Valley and Rout 128*, Cambridge, MA: Harvard University Press.

Saxenian, AnnLee (1999), *Silicon Valley's New Immigrant Entrepreneurs*, Berkeley, CA: Public Policy Institute of California.

Schultz, Theodore W. (1971), *Investment in Human Capital: The Role of Education and Research*, London: Free Press.

Schumpeter, Joseph (1939), *Business Cycles: A*

Theoretical, Historical, and Statistical Analysis of the Capitalist Process, New York: McGraw-Hill.

Schumpeter, Joseph (1942), *Capitalism, Socialism and Democracy*, New York: Harper & Brothers.

Scott, Allan (1993), *Technopolis: High-Technology Industry and Regional Development in Southern California*, Berkeley, CA: University of California Press.

Shachar, Ari and Sture Öberg (eds) (1990), *The World Economy and the Spatial Organization of Power*, Aldershot: Avebury.

Simonton, Dean Keith (2006), 'Creativity around the world in 80 ways . . . but with one destination', in Kaufman, James and Sternberg, Robert (eds), *The International Handbook of Creativity*, New York: Cambridge University Press.

Smith, Gudmund (1990), 'Testad kreativitet', in Klein, Georg (ed.), *Om krativitet och flow*, Stockholm: Brombergs.

Smith, Gudmund and Ingegerd Carlsson (1990), 'The creative process: a functional model based on empirical studies from early childhood to middle age', *Psychological Issues, Monograph 57*. New York: International Universities Press.

Sörlin, Sverker and Gunnar Törnqvist (2000), *Kunskap för välstånd. Universiteten och omvandlingen av Sverige*, Stockholm: SNS Förlag.

Sörlin, Sverker and Gunnar Törnqvist (2006), 'Universitet och regioner – ett återbesök', in Kjell Blückert and Eva Österberg (eds), *Gränslöst –forskning i Sverige och i världen. Festskift till Dan Brändström*, Stockholm: Naturoch Kultur.

Storper, Michael (1989), 'The transition to flexible specialisation in the U.S. film industry: external economies, the division of labor, and crossing industrial divides', *Cambridge Journal of Economics*, **13**.

Ström, G. (ed.), *Erövra universiteten åter*, Stockholm: Liber.

Tatsuno, S.M. (1986), *The Technopolis Strategy: Japan, High Technology, and the Control of the Twenty-first Century*, New York: Prentice-Hall Press.

Thomson, W. (1965), 'Bureaucracy and innovation', *Administrative Science Quarterly*, **10**(1).

Thufvesson, Ola (2006), *Kreativitetens yttre villkor. Miljöer, rörlighet och nobelpristagare.* Lund: Institutionen för kulturgeografi och ekonomisk geografi.

Törnqvist, Gunnar (1983), 'Kreativitetens geografi', *Svensk Geografisk Årsbok*, Lund: Gleerup.

Törnqvist, Gunnar (1989), 'La Créativité: Une Perspective Géographique', *La Géographie de la Créativité et de l'Innovation*, Paris: Université de Paris-Sorbonne.

Törnqvist, Gunnar (1990), 'Towards a geography of creativity', in Ari Shachar and Sture Öberg (eds), *The World Economy and the Spatial Organization of Power*, Aldershot, UK: Avebury.

Törnqvist, Gunnar (1998), *Renässans för regioner. Om tekniken och den sociala kommunikationens villkor*, Stockholm: SNS Förlag.

Törnqvist, Gunnar (2002), *Science at the Cutting Edge. The Future of the Øresund Region*,

Köpenhamn, Denmark: Copenhagen Business School Press.

Törnqvist, Gunnar (2004), 'Creativity in time and space', *Geografiska Annaler*, **86 B**.

Törnqvist, Gunnar (2004), *Kreativitetens geografi*, Stockholm: SNS Förlag.

Törnqvist, Gunnar (2009), *Kreativitet i tid och rum – processer, personer och platser*, Stockholm: SNS Förlag.

Torrence, E.P. (1962), *Guiding Creative Talent*, Englewood Cliffs, NJ: Prentice-Hall;

Torrence, E.P. (1974), *The Torrence Test of Creative Thinking*, Bensenville, IL: Scholastic Testing Service.

Tson Söderström, Hans (ed.) (2001), *Kluster.se Sverige i den nya ekonomiska geografin*, Stockholm: SNS Förlag.

Universiteten och forskningen – en vision. Utmaningar och problem. Forskningsstrategiska utskottet, Kungl. Vetenskapsakademien, 2008.

Wallas, Graham (1926), *Art of Thought*, New York: Harcourt Brace.

Weisberg, Robert W. (1993), *Beyond the Myth of Genius*, New York: Freeman.

Westlund, Hans and Roger Bolton (2003), 'Local social capital and entrepreneurship', *Small Business Economics*, **21**.

Wikhall, Maria (2001), *Universiteten och kompetenslandskapet. Effekter av den högre utbildningens tillväxt och regionala spridning i Sverige*, Lund: Institutionen för kulturgeografi och ekonomisk geografi, Lunds universitet.

Useful Websites

http://www.cwts.nl/cwts/LR The Leiden
   Ranking
http://ed.sjtu.edu.en/rank/2007 Academic
   Ranking of World Universities
http://en.wikipedia.org/wiki/Nokia
http://www.nobelprize.org
http://scientific.thomsonreuters.com
http://topuniversities.com/home/.Times
   Higher Education Supplement (THES)

Index

academic entrepreneur 24, 113, 160
Academic Ranking of World-Universities 102
Academy, Gk Akademeia 27, 120
Acropolis 27
Aerospace Alley 85
Aeschylus 27
agora 24, 41
Alexander the Great 28
Alexandria 28–9
Analogy 12, 74
analytic sources of knowledge 89
Andersson, Åke E. 47
apex university 149
Archimedes 9, 10, 28
Archimedes´ principle 10
Arezzo 56
Aristarchos 29
Aristotle 27
Arno, River 31
aroma of creativity 125, 173
artist collectives 165
Athens 26–9, 40, 42, 161
Athenaeum (dining room) 110
Austin 53
Austro-Hungarian Empire 32, 43, 175

Bach, Johann Sebastian 21
Balkanized culture (Vienna) 44
Bárány, Robert 33
Basel Institut für Immunologi 106
Bayer, chemical company 38
Beach, Sylvia 35

Beauvoir, Simone de 35
Becker, Garry 111, 150–51
Beckett, Samuel 35
Békésy, George 156
Bell, Clive 36
Bell, Vanessa 36
Berlin 33–5, 39, 40, 41, 42, 44, 64, 138, 140, 147, 162, 165
bibliometric analysis 103, 170
bifurcation zone 74
bisociation 7–8
bisociative chock effect 8
Bloomsbury (London) 36, 44
Bloomsbury Group 35–6
Bohemian index 52
Bohr, Margarethe 122
Bohr, Niels 106–7, 111, 121
Bologna 30, 56
Boltzmann, Ludwig 33
Bono, Edward de 12–13
Born, Max 107
Boston 39, 40, 53, 64, 138, 162, 165
brain drain 138–9
Bright, John 37
British Museum 36
Broadway Musical Industry (BMI) 115
Brod, Max 34
Brunelleschi, Filippo 30
Budapest 138, 147, 154–5, 175
Buchanan, James 111
bureaucracy 67, 69
Burton, Nina 3, 45
business climate 59
business cycles 22

cafes of *fin de siècle* Vienna 41
California Institute of
    Technology (Cal Tech) 72,
    85, 108–10
Cambridge 36, 85
Cambridge University *see*
    University of Cambridge
Camus, Albert 35
Canetti, Elias 32
Carpi 56
Castells, Manuel 38, 78
Catholic Church 56
Cederlund, Kerstin 49
Centennial exhibition (Nobel
    Prize) 130
CERN, The European
    Laboratory for Particle
    Physics 105
Chagall, Marc 34
chaos 42–3, 156
chartism 37
Chicago 138, 147
Chicago School of Economics
    111, 151
city-regions (urban regions,
    metropolitan areas) 59
city-state 28, 31, 56, 155, 161
civility 56
cluster 87–90
Coase, Ronald 111, 150
co-authorship 112, 115
Cobden, Richard 37
codified knowledge 91–2, 118
Cold Spring Harbor Laboratory
    107
Cold War 80, 83, 86
Columbus, Christopher 29
convergent thinking 7, 160,
    179
converce 120
conversation 120
con-verso (Lat.) 120
Copenhagen 107, 121
Copenhagener spirit 107
creare (Lat.) 2
creative, creativity
    definitions 1–2

creative capital 50, 58, 61, 66
creative child 17–18
creative class 18, 51, 160
creative destruction 22
créativité (Fr.) 1
creativity, four Ps of (product,
    process, person, and place)
    3–6
creativity index 53
creator
    the groundbreaking 23
    the original 20
Cronin, James W. 146–7
cross-fertilisation 61
cultural web (fabric) 50
Curie, Marie 111

Dallas 53, 147
Dalton, John 37
Darwin, Charles 112
Delbrück, Max 107
Democritus 128
Department of Social and
    Economic Geography,
    Lund University 141
Detroit 91
dialogue 120
dichotomy 178
Dirac, Paul 107
discovery 1
divergent thinking 7, 160,
    179
dynamic force fields 178–80

egalitarian (flat) organizations
    66, 68, 69 123, 167, 172
Einstein, Albert 34, 107, 111,
    112, 122, 146–7
Emilia-Romagna 56
Engels, Friedrich 37
entrepreneur 22–3, 25–6, 31, 51,
    62, 86, 87, 93, 129, 132, 139,
    160, 177, 181–2
Eratosthenes 28–9
Erdös, Paul 154
Esbo 72
escalator region 50

escalator university 149
'eureka' (Gk 'heureka') 9
Euripides 27

Fiorina, Carley 51
Fitzgerald, Scott 35
flat (egalitarian) organization
    66, 68
Flexner, Simon 109, 125
Florens 29–31, 40, 42, 64, 161,
    165
Florida, Richard 18–9, 50–58
Fogel, Robert 111, 150
food and health-care industries
    81
Forster, Edward Morgan 36
forum 41
France, Anatole 34
French Revolution 43
Freud, Sigmund 7, 21, 32
Friedman, Milton 111, 150
Fry, Roger 36

Galilei, Galileo 112
Gay index 52
Geneva 105
genius 1
geographic mobility 164
Gide, André 35
Giotto di Bondone 30
grammar school 156
grand tours 139
Grant, Duncan 36
Greater Greece 128
Grenoble 105
growth pole 90
Guilford, J.P. 7, 12
Gutenberg, Johann 9–12
Gymnasium 27, 147, 153, 156,
    175
Göttingen 37, 40, 148, 162
Göttinger Vereinung 38

Hägerstrand, Torsten 128,
    141–2
Hall, Peter 39, 47
Hamburg 138

Hamsun, Knut 34
Hargittai, István 134–5
Harvard University 102, 137
health-care industries 81
Heisenberg, Werner 107, 121
Hellas 28
Hellenism 28, 40
Helsinki 72
Helsinki University of
    Technology 72
Hemingway, Ernest 35
Hertz, Heinrich 33
hierarchical organizations 65,
    68–9, 81, 123, 166–7, 172
Highway 128 complex 185
Hitler, Adolf 34, 147, 176
Hollingsworth, Rogers 108,
    122–3, 125
Hollywood (Hollywood
    concept) 54, 91
'Homo ludens' 18
horizontal job market 54
Houston 53
human capital 19, 55, 61, 66

Idéon, Research Park 73
illumination, phase of creative
    process 15
incubation, phase of creative
    process 15
infrastructure
    cultural 48, 49, 164
    physical 47
innovation 2
    economic innovation 22
    product innovation 22
    process innovation 22
innovation systems 87–91
innovative ability 2
innovator 161, 168
Institute for Advanced Study,
    Princeton 148
Institute for Theoretical
    Physics, Copenhagen 107
Institute of Higher Education,
    Shanghai Jiao Tong
    University 99

Institut für physikalischen Chemie und Elektrochemie, Göttingen 38
Institut Laue-Langevin 105
Institut Pasteur, Paris 105
intellectual geometry 8
interactive learning 89
invention 1, 21, 22, 87
inventor 161
invisible colleges, universities 116, 170
Ionia 28

Jacob, François 105
Jacobs, Jane 58
Jerne, Niels 106
Jewish emigrants 140
Jewish homes 152
Jewish mothers 152
Jewish Nobel laureates 152
Joule, James Prescott 37
journeyman system 139
Joyce, James 35
Jung, Carl Gustav 32

Kafka, Franz 34
Kaiser-Wilhelm-Institut für Physik, Berlin 34, 148
Kaliningrad (Königsberg) 144
Kandinsky, Wassily 34
Kant, Immanuel 144
Karolinska Institutet 71, 101, 130, 133, 152
keeper, academic 93, 161
Keynes, John Maynard 36
keystone 14
Kista-Arlanda corridor 85
Klein, Felix 38, 150
Klein, Georg 152
Klimt, Gustav 32
knowledge based economy 19, 47, 70, 79, 88
Koestler, Arthur 7–8, 12, 154
Kokoschka, Oskar 32, 34
Königsberg (Kaliningrad) 144
Koopmans, Tjalling 111, 150

'Kopenhagener Geist, Der' 107
Kraus, Karl 33, 34
Krupp, Alfred 38

Lagerlöf, Selma 34
Landry, Charles 48
Landsteiner, Karl 33
lateral thinking 12–14
Leiden Ranking, The 100
Leonardo da Vinci 30
life path 143, 145–8
Lindqvist, Svante 135
lingua franca 101
linear model 88
London 33, 35–6, 39, 40, 41, 42, 64, 73, 138, 162, 165
London-Heathrow-Reading corridor 85
Loos, Adolf 32
Lorenz, Konrad 33
Los Alamos National Laboratory (LANL) 44
Lost Generation 35
Lucas, Robert 111, 115, 151
Luceum, Gk Lykeion 27
Lund 49, 73
Lund University *see* University of Lund
Lutheran Gymnasium, Budapest 154–5
lycée 156

Maffia, The 56
Macedonia 28
Mahler, Gustav 32
Manchester 36–7, 40, 42, 44, 162
Manchester Liberalism 37
Manhattan Project 80
Mann, Heinrich 34
Markowitz, Harry 111, 150
Massachusetts Institute of Technology 72, 85, 88
see also MIT
Medici, the family 31, 40
metropolis 46, 163–5
Michelangelo Buonarotti 30

military-industrial complex 81
Miller, Henry 35
Miller, Merton 111, 150
Minta Gymnasium, Budapest
    154–5
MIT *see* Massachusetts Institute
    of Technology
modernism 33
Monnier, Adrienne 35
Moore, George Edward 36
Mozart, Wolfgang Amadeus
    20, 21
MRC Laboratory of Molecular-
    Biology, Cambridge 138
Munich 85, 138
Museion 29

Nernst, Walther 38
network milieux 112–6
network theory 114
Neumann, John von 154–5
New York 39, 40, 53, 64, 138,
    162, 165
Newton, Isaac 11, 112
Nobel, Alfred
    Alfred Nobel´s will 129–30
Nobel Foundation 130
Nobel laureates 129–40, 145–8,
    170, 173
Nobel Museum 134, 135, 145
Nobel Prize 130–31
Nokia Corporation 72
Norén, Lars 42

oil crisis of *1973–74* 83
Oldenburg, Ray 54
Oresund Region 71
Österberg, Eva 97
Oxford 105
Oxford English Dictionary, The 1

Padua 30
Palo Alto 72
Paris 33, 34–6, 40, 41, 42, 44, 64,
    129, 138, 140, 162, 165
Pasteur, Louis 105
Pasteur Institute of Paris 105

Pauli, Wolfgang 107
Pauling, Linus 110
peer-review 96, 115, 170
Pentagon 83
people climate 59
Perroux, François 90
Piaristorden Gymnasium,
    Budapest 154
piazza 41
pioneer 24, 25, 31, 51, 70, 77, 87,
    93, 129, 132, 139, 152, 160,
    168, 177, 181–2
Pireus 42
Pisa 30
Pitti, the family 40
Plateau de Saclay 85
Plato 27, 120
playfulness and discipline 128,
    180
Poincaré, Henri 14
'pôle de croissance' (growth
    pole) 90
Popper, Karl 20–21
Porter, Michael 90
Pound, Ezra 35
Prague 138
preparation, phase of creative
    process 15
Preston, Pascal 39, 180
Prigogine, Ilya 45, 180
Princeton University *see*
    University of Princeton
printing press 11–12
Prize in Economic Sciences in
    Memory of Alfred Nobel
    see Sveriges Riksbank
    Prize
Protagoras 27
proximity
    in networks 48
    territorial, physical 48, 88
Ptolemy 28
publish-or-perish-syndrom 95
Putnam, Robert D. 56
Pythagoras 28

Quantum physics 111

Rafael (Raffaelo Santi) 30
Raleigh-Durham 53
ranking of universities 98–103,
   169
regional innovation system 91
Renaissance 29
Rockefeller Institute,
   Rockefeller University
   108–10, 125
Rome 30, 56
rookies 114, 116
Rosenberg, Nathan 89
Royal Swedish Academy of
   Sciences, The 95, 110, 124,
   130–31, 133
Rue de la Bûcherie 35
Rue de l'Odéon 35
Russell, Bertrand 36
Rutherford Appleton
   Laboratory 105
Russian bookstores 34
Russian emigrants 33, 140
Russian newspapers 34
Russian publishing houses 34
Russian Revolution 33, 43, 140

Sahlin, Nils-Eric 20, 124
St Petersburg 44
Samos 29
San Diego 53
San Francisco 53, 64, 165
San Remo 129
Sartre, Jean-Paul 35
Sassuolo 56
Schrödinger, Erwin 107, 121–2
Schultz, Theodore W. 55, 111,
   115
Schumpeter, Joseph A. 22, 33,
   87
Schönberg, Arnold 32
Science (journal) 114, 116
Seattle 53
Shakespeare, William 1
Shakespeare and Company
   (bookstore in Paris) 35
Sicily 28
Siemens, Werner von 38

Silicon Valley 44, 52, 72, 85, 91
Smith, Adam 55
Smith, Gudmund 19
social capital 55–8, 66
socially distributed 82
social web (fabric) 57
Socrates 27, 120
Södertälje 71
Solvay Conferences 111
Sony Ericsson Mobile
   Communications 73
Sophia Antipolis 85
Sophocles 27
Soros, George 154
space research programs 80,
   86
stable phase of development
   74–7
Stagnelius, Erik Johan 42
Stanford University *see*
   University of Stanford
stations in time and space 142,
   148
Stein, Gertrud 35
Stiegler, George 111
Stockholm 71
Stony Brook University 147
Storper, Michael 54
structural instability 43, 156
Sturm, Der 34
Sveriges Riksbank Prize in
   Economic Sciences in
   Memory of Alfred Nobel
   55, 110, 131, 150
Syene 29
synergie 85–6
synthetic knowledgebase 89
Szegö, Gabriel 154

tacit knowledge 91–2
Tampere University of
   Technology 72
teacher´s competence and
   inspirational abilities 153
technology, talent and
   tolerance 51–2
technological cluster 89

technological system 89
Teller, Edward 155
Third Italy 56
third mission 83–4
third place 54
Thomson Reuters 96
time filter 144
Time-geography 141–5, 174
Times Higher Education QS 100
track-bound development 61
trajectory 142
Tsukuba 85

Uccello, Paolo 30
Uleåborg 72
Ulm 147
University College London 36
University of
    Cambridge 72, 88, 107, 138, 169, 176
    Chicago 55, 111, 150
    Colombia 147
    Copenhagen 71, 101
    Glasgow 72
    Helsinki 72
    Leiden 100
    London 36
    Lund 19, 71, 97, 101, 128
    Oxford 169, 176
    Princeton 146–8
    Uppsala 49, 71

Wisconsin 108
Zurich 148
unstable phase of development 74–7

Veneto 56
Venice 31
verification, phase of creative process 15
vertical thinking 12–4
veterans 114, 116
Vienna 32–3, 40, 41, 42, 43, 64, 138, 162, 165

Wagner, Otto 32
Wagner-Jauregg, Julius 33
Walden, Herwarth 34
Wallas, Graham 14
Washington-Baltimore 53
Web of Science 96
Weininger, Otto 32
Weisberg, Robert 21
Whitehead, Alfred North 1
Wigner, Eugene 146–7
Wittgenstein, Ludwig 20–21
Woolf, Virginia 36
World Trade Center (11 September 2001) 83

Yang, Chen Ning 146–7

Zürich patent office 147